M000028345

yes,
I *do*
exist

To the Zegan
Family —
Best Wishes!

Mike

yes, I do exist

Shark2th

Yes, I Do Exist
Copyright © 2019 by Shark2th

Library of Congress Control Number: 2018954009
ISBN-13:   Paperback: 978-1-64398-184-0
                PDF: 978-1-64398-185-7
                ePub: 978-1-64398-186-4
                Kindle   978-1-64398-187-1

Printed in the United States of America

LitFire LLC
1-800-511-9787
www.litfirepublishing.com
order@litfirepublishing.com

Contents

ACKNOWLEDGMENTS

All through my life, I have been blessed to meet so many outstanding people. You have all contributed to the man that I am. Through conversations and interactions, I have learned from each and every one of you. Whether it be friends, co-workers, business interactions, leisure activities, or relationships—I treasure you all. I hope that most human beings attain the feelings that life has brought to me.

I have often said, "I have acquired my skills and knowledge because I have had great teachers throughout my life."

I owe a great debt of gratitude to the personnel of the United States Military, the U.S. government, and its many institutions.

My sincere thanks to all the worldwide friends who have given me encouragement to tell my story and write this book over the last few years, especially Silvia Olivetti, Jeff Sihilling, Jean Marc Dorckel, and Danny Sullivan.

As this book neared completion, special thanks go to my mother, my son, Mark Dougan, and Jerrie Newman.

I dedicate this book in loving memory of

Cathy D.

my father, Clarence

my brother, Richard

*"When it is all said and done, what we leave behind
is what we left; not what we left out."*

PREFACE

This book revolves around two separate days of my life—one in December of 1990, and the other in May of 1991. The chapters of this book that contain peripheral background leading up to those pivotal days have been significantly abbreviated in order not to detract from the primary storyline. The events contained within are true, and all conversations are verbatim to the best of my recollection. I have tried to avoid using people's names for reasons that will become apparent to the reader, and my story has not been embellished or exaggerated in any way.

Many who read this story will consider it a work of fiction—and I can understand that. But for those who are willing to accept it as the factual account that it is, I believe the experiences contained herein will motivate many to reach higher in life and reduce the conditioning that binds the evolution of our species.

All human beings are products of their environment and experiences. Many never discover their own unique gifts or attributes because they do not push themselves beyond their perceived or conditioned limits. Traumatic experiences also factor into the realization that impossible things can be accomplished. My point here is that mankind as a whole is both suppressed and confined by the preconceptions and limits dictated, or rather conditioned, by civilization, society, and history. Once these limiting beliefs are set aside, many things thought and taught to be impossible will be accomplished.

This book centers around my experiences in relation to the interaction with institutions of the United States government and its personnel over two particular days. I feel that it is important for the reader to know that there are many debatable reasons why the United States government and Department of Defense felt it best that the world not know of my existence. I was never asked to sign any agreement of non-disclosure for I hold no governmental secrets. The fact is that, as they stated, I am the secret.

I have what I call a semi-videographic memory. I vividly remember many events that have affected my life as if I were playing them back in a video recording. Over twenty-five years have passed since the events of this book took place, yet my recollection of what happened and the near verbatim dialogue between myself and others can be verified by video surveillance taken at the time—but these recordings have been deemed classified by the Department of Defense.

I hope that many of the exceptional people I met during this period of time run across this book and take the time to read it; if they do, they will be able to corroborate the accuracy of this account.

CHAPTER 1

DEFCON 4

The pre-dawn tranquility of the White House in Washington D.C. is broken at 3:00 a.m. by a phone call. It is early December 1990, a few weeks prior to Operation Desert Storm of the Gulf War, which is being planned in complete secrecy.

The Director of the CIA has awakened the President from his sleep to inform him that the United States Military is at DEFCON 4. Strategic Air Command has scrambled B-2 bomber squadrons into the air, but there are no designated targets. They do not know who the enemy is or which country (or countries) may be involved.

The Director proceeds to tell the President that a foreign military spy has just successfully infiltrated the United States Military and has completely shut down the most secure super-computer system in the world, the recently installed Department of Defense mainframe. Every NORAD missile defense screen in all secure military installations in the country has gone dark, and the United States of America is extremely vulnerable to attack from any direction.

When the President demands to know how an enemy has subdued the defense system of the most powerful country on the planet, the Director explains that a thirty-one-year-old enlistee in the U.S. Navy has just achieved a perfect score on the ASVAP entrance examination, then states, "Everyone knows it is impossible to get a perfect score on the ASVAP. This foreign agent was fed answers to the test by electronic means, which we could not detect. When his test was graded by the

Department of Defense mainframe computer, it shut itself down and issued an error message that someone had achieved a perfect score. The technicians and security personnel assure me that this was never programmed into the system."

Having just awakened, the President takes a minute to gather his thoughts about the urgency of the military defensive situation and the facts presented to him. He comments to his CIA advisor, "If we could not detect that any electronic means were used, you have no real evidence that this is the case. Maybe this man actually is this smart..."

The President then orders the Director of the CIA to immediately wake up the Directors of the NSA and FBI. He wants all three Directors onboard Air Force One within the hour for "wheels up." They are all flying to Oakland, California, to meet this man. The Director advises the President that such an action is not within normal protocol as the United States is technically at war, and the President should not leave the security of the White House.

The President insists that his orders be followed. The cross-country flight aboard Air Force One will take several hours. Arrival time on the west coast will be sometime after 8:00 a.m. Pacific time.

This is the first time in United States history that a president has left his post as Commander in Chief during a war and made an unscheduled flight to meet an enlisted man, or anyone else for that matter.

CHAPTER 2

THE HIGHWAY OF LIFE

Life is an untraveled road opening before you. Seldom do your plans or directions take the path you anticipate. Decisions are made along the way, most of which cannot be undone. We all make mistakes and poor choices at times. This is simply human nature and the method by which we learn and live. The goal becomes making better choices and not repeating mistakes. Consistency, determination, and sheer will become the primary driving forces to move forward and navigate the unexpected.

Throughout life we all make many friends and acquaintances, some seemingly by accident. Personally, I feel that there are no accidents in life. Paths are meant to cross, roads are meant to be shared. The same is true of emotions and events experienced as well.

We all have lost or will lose loved ones throughout our lifetime. These losses affect our disposition and behavior, sometimes traumatically, sometimes for years. We must stay strong and struggle through the healing process. Others need the friendship and love that we have to share. I believe this is actually what makes us human beings.

Compassion, love, honesty, and truth are qualities I feel mankind has begun to lose over the course of time. The modern world is conditioned psychologically by the concepts of society, civilization, and wealth—all fabricated along the way of evolution, when the roots of life are so much simpler and so much more important.

We live and learn, we try and fail, we continue and succeed. Our directions are diverse from one perspective, but so intertwined from others.

In the late 1970s, after high school, I attended Ventura and Moorpark Colleges. My courses included the basic requirements for math, science, English, etc.—core classes that would transfer to a California university once I decided which university I wanted to attend and what I wanted to study.

I had a deep interest in marine biology, oceanography, and plate tectonics, mainly influenced by my surfing so much. I felt in tune with the ocean and nature. I was at peace while bobbing gently in the ocean's rhythmic swells, sometimes for hours, waiting for big sets on smaller days.

My father, a physicist with a degree from MIT, felt I should pursue a degree in computer science. That field was experiencing a technological explosion and was likely to grow exponentially over the next several decades. In those days, computer cards were in use, and the floppy disc was new technology. Silicon chips were becoming smaller and smaller each year, and computing ability was beginning to boom. The technology contained in my iPad today would have taken up a whole building at that time.

I decided to attend Cal Poly in San Luis Obispo, California, since it was becoming renowned as the top computer science school in the country. Another plus was that one of my younger brothers would be attending their School of Architecture as soon as he graduated from high school. The final deciding factor was its proximity to Hazards Canyon, a surf spot on the coast just west of San Luis Obispo. At that time, it was a secret spot known to local surfers for huge, powerful, hollow waves of the same caliber as the big waves in Hawaii or Indonesia. If I was going to study hard at school, I knew I needed a place where I could release tension and experience the big wave adrenaline to keep me psychologically balanced.

On the coast of California south of Point Conception, the big northern swells are blocked by the Santa Barbara Islands. The coastline heads east-southeast, and these swells bend and lose some of their energy. But going north from Point Conception, the continental shelf is narrower, allowing raw, deep ocean swells to carry their energy closer to the shoreline before being affected by the drag of shallower water.

After a couple of years of junior college, I transferred to Cal Poly and spent my first summer quarter with a friend named Todd from high school, renting a room in his house. I started that summer with a full twelve-unit class load in order to set my pace for the coming year, but the study load was not too heavy because my high school education overlapped course material in physics, math, and chemistry.

When the fall quarter started, I moved into an apartment with three great guys, Dale, Barry, and Pat. They were all graphics art majors, and each had a different concentration within the field. Watching my roommates doing their art projects was a huge influence on me. I was an artist at heart too. I yearned to build more surfboards as I interacted daily with these three incredibly talented young men. We were all very close in age.

My roommate Pat was from Huntington Beach. In his younger years, he was an NSSA surfing champion. We surfed together when we could, which was very frequently. He taught me the ropes of all the local breaks, pushing me to surf better and feel confident in the seasonally huge surf of the Central Coast winter months. He introduced me to the secret surf spots along the Big Sur coastline.

School was okay, but I began ditching classes when the waves were big. I was surfing almost as much as I was going to class. I was still doing well on tests, though my instructors would occasionally comment on my wet hair and the salt crystals on my face as I entered classes right on time for tests.

Then everything changed on Valentine's Day. My friend Greg and I had gone up to a bar in the town of Cayucos, north of San Luis Obispo. Not many single women were there, but Greg kept buying beers because he really liked the band and wanted to hang out and listen to them. As we took the back way home from Morro Bay, he asked me how fast my Karmann Ghia could go. I was demonstrating when I broke loose in a curve at almost 100 miles per hour after we exited the freeway. Neither of us was hurt, but my car was severely damaged. It was running, but I couldn't drive away because all the Porsche alloy wheels were shattered. Greg hitchhiked out before the police arrived, and I went to jail for the night.

My life had flashed before my eyes during the accident. I thought deeply about my direction in life. I wanted to build surfboards. I was good enough to be a professional shaper and manufacturer. I made the decision to drop out of school, though I didn't tell my parents for months.

I moved into a very small ranch house with two other surfing friends from Ventura; the rent was cheap and we were halfway between town and the beach. I converted an old chicken coop into a shaping room and started building custom surfboards for close friends.

When my parents found out what I had done, my father almost disowned me. He was upset that I didn't tell them about the auto accident or dropping out of college, and he told me I should be ashamed for setting such a poor example for all five of my younger siblings. The son of a farmer in Mississippi, he had become a top electro-optics physicist for the Department of Defense. In his mind, as well as in the minds of most in my generation and his, success in life required a college degree. To me, this is a psychologically programmed ideal of society and civilization. While an education is necessary, it is like wealth—absolutely no gauge of a human being's worth or abilities. It is but a purchased piece of paper.

A year and a half later, I was a partner in the only legitimate and licensed surfboard factory between Santa Barbara and Santa Cruz. Lots of guys built boards, and many were exceptional shapers and builders; but our factory was legal and licensed to manufacture surfboards.

With a 2,400-square-foot steel building and filtration systems for dust and fumes, we were licensed to have 55-gallon drums of flammable materials. We pumped out custom boards weekly, offering a two-week turnaround time and reduced prices. We threw in custom two-color airbrushed paint jobs for free. We did boat and car fiberglass repairs on the side, and friends that needed help with almost anything would just stop by the factory. Then my partner and I had some differences a few years down the road. We split up, but to this day, I still consider him one of the most respected and cherished friends in my life.

Shortly after our split, I moved in with four surfing buddies who were Cuesta Junior College students. They all surfed, and three of them worked construction. I slept on their couch until I found work in construction. When one roommate moved out, I took his room and started building limited custom surfboards out of the garage.

In the summer of 1984, a roommate's girlfriend introduced me to her friend Cathy, who had moved up to the Central Coast from Glendale in southern California. Cathy was attending Cuesta Junior College and was twenty years old. Half Italian and half Spanish, she was simply beautiful. *Gorgeous* was an understatement; *perfection* better described how I felt about her. We dated for a few months, but I felt it best to stop since she was about five years younger than I was.

After we stopped dating, I frequently saw Cathy at parties or at the beach; quite a few of our mutual friends surfed together often. I remember one barbecue party in the summer of 1985 in particular. It was late evening at a surfing buddy's house on the beach near Cayucos, north of Morro Bay. I recall sitting on the couch talking to a pretty blonde named Betsy who was friends with both Cathy and me. She had asked me to dance, but I had just opened a fresh imported beer and so had she. I saw Cathy standing across the living room talking to three or four guys from her school.

Betsy asked, "Why did you and Cathy stop seeing each other?"

I replied that I felt Cathy should get through college and she would probably be better off dating guys from school since I had dropped out of college a few years before and was just building surfboards and working construction.

Betsy said very seriously, "You're a smart guy, but you're an idiot!"

I thought, "What prompted that comment?"

She continued, "You don't see the way she looks at you, but I see the way she looks at you when you aren't looking. Do you even realize the way you look at her when she isn't watching? We women see these things. You two belong together! You know it and she knows it, and you both try to play this stupid bullshit game of trying to ignore each other.

You need to go ask her out, or I am going to embarrass the heck out of you right now!"

Betsy was right. I had been in love with Cathy since the day I first saw her. Our first kiss, over a year earlier, could have lasted a lifetime. In my whole life, I had never felt so deeply drawn to anyone. No one since had ever felt as right as Cathy did in my arms.

Just at that moment, Betsy yelled out, "Cathy, get your ass over here!"

I said, "Betsy, what are you doing?"

Cathy walked over, and Betsy told her to have a seat on the couch. As Cathy started to sit on the other side of Betsy, Betsy grabbed her arm and swung her down next to me. Cathy plopped down on the couch right beside me with such momentum that she almost bounced into my lap.

Betsy started in with a really loud voice, "I am sick and tired of watching this bullshit! Look at each other. Now, either of you tell me that the two of you don't belong together."

Cathy and I were both pretty embarrassed as the room went silent except for the background music. People stared at the three of us sitting on the couch, waiting for some response.

Betsy remarked to the room in general, "Mind your own business, people!" She turned to us and said, "Nothing to say? Neither of you is shy, so I want to hear it. Still no answer? Then you two better start dating again, or I am going to smack you both!"

Cathy and I couldn't stop laughing as she asked Betsy if she was drunk.

Betsy said something like, "If I were drunk, I would never have called you over here and I would be all over him; so you better hang on to him, girl! I have never seen two people more in love trying to avoid admitting it to themselves. The way the two of you look at each other from across the room makes me horny! Excuse me while I go find my own guy."

We were laughing so hard as Betsy walked away, smiling at the two of us. I took Cathy's hand, and we walked out to the bonfire on the beach.

Cathy said, "She's so funny, but she's right. Why do we do this?"

"I guess I'm afraid because of the way I feel about you. I have never felt so right with anyone," I said.

She replied with, "I guess that makes two of us."

We kissed passionately for several minutes. After that night, we saw each other nearly every day and went out several times a week. Life felt good, and I couldn't have been any happier.

One Sunday in November of 1985, Cathy and I had gone out to dinner at our favorite restaurant, the Great American Fish Company in Morro Bay. We had a few drinks with dinner—actually, it was a bottle of wine with dinner and a few shots of Tuacca after dinner.

When we got back to her apartment, we stood outside next to my old Toyota truck, kissing. I felt like no one else in the world existed, it was just the two of us. After about half an hour, she told me her roommate was gone for the night and asked me to stay with her. Then all of a sudden she asked, "How much money do you have in your pocket?"

I told her that I had only about $350 left after rent and bills, but I would get another good paycheck on Friday. She told me she only had about $80 left after her bills.

I asked, "Do you need some money? You don't have to pay me back."

She surprised me with, "Do you think we have enough money to drive to Vegas right now and get married? We can take my car. I just had it tuned up last week."

I paused, sort of overwhelmed, as I looked into her brown eyes, "Cathy, you have classes tomorrow and I have to work at 8:00. Besides, we haven't even met each other's families yet. If we are going to get married, we need to do this right."

"But I love you, and I know I never want to be with anyone else ever again but you," she said as she looked deep into my eyes.

"You know I have loved only you since the moment I first saw you, but let's not rush things. We have our whole lives to be together."

As she said, "Okay, you're right," she grabbed my hand as we headed into her apartment, where we both promptly passed out. We didn't even get out of our clothes. When my watch alarm went off at 7:00 a.m., Cathy woke up as well. We both felt a little hung over from the Tuacca, and I asked her if she remembered the previous night's conversation.

She said, "Of course I do! You didn't want to drive to Vegas and marry me."

"That is not what happened!" I said in a serious voice.

"I know; I love you. I just wanted to see your reaction," she replied with light laughter.

"I gotta get to work, you gotta get to school, so I'll call you later tonight. I can't be late." I kissed her deeply and held her tightly, not wanting to leave, and headed out the door. I recall co-workers asking me why I was in such a great mood that day.

That week we had less than our usual contact as Cathy was called in to work extra shifts several nights. She worked part-time as a cocktail waitress and hostess at a nice restaurant near Avilla Beach, a thirty mile drive south of where we lived.

When Friday came along, I asked my boss if I could take an extra half hour for lunch to take care of something important. I was always ahead of schedule with my work, so he had no problem agreeing. I drove to the local florist and ordered a dozen long-stemmed red roses to be sent to Cathy's apartment. On the card I wrote:

Dinner this evening?
I'll call you after work.
I LOVE YOU!

The rest of the afternoon at work went by quickly. I got paid and headed home. I shared a four-bedroom house with three other surfers who also were construction workers and college students. They were all a few years younger than me, and two of them grew up in the same town that Cathy did. Vicky, the girl who had introduced Cathy and me, was visiting her boyfriend, one of my roommates. Vicky would often spend weeks or months at a time living in the house with our roommate. We often had friends spending extended periods of time with us. It was a surf house; I built and repaired surfboards in the garage in my free time.

I tried to call Cathy just after sunset, but no one was home. About an hour later, I was able to reach her roommate. She told me Cathy had been called in to work an extra evening shift again. She said that Cathy loved the roses I had sent and was excited to see me when she got off work, if it wasn't too late. She closed our conversation with, "I wish my boyfriend sent me red roses once in awhile!"

I took a shower and had a couple of beers with the guys as we sat around the living room telling surf stories and watching home videos of ourselves surfing. One of my roommates had a nice video camera set-up that he took to the beach with us frequently.

I called Cathy's roommate again who said she had talked to Cathy at work a short while before. Cathy was angry that she had been called in to work because it wasn't busy. Her roommate told me that the owners of the restaurant had been trying to get her drunk to try to take advantage of her, and Cathy wanted to leave.

I was angry. I should have driven down to the restaurant right then. I asked Cathy's roommate to call her back at work and tell Cathy to quit work, and I would support her through school. Her roommate called me back a few minutes later, saying that Cathy had quit her job and was coming directly to pick me up at my house because she just wanted to see me, and we didn't have to go out anywhere.

After an hour passed, I started to worry. Vicky asked when Cathy was supposed to be coming by, and I told her she should have arrived by now. Several minutes later, the telephone rang and Vicky answered it. Vicky broke into tears, and her boyfriend rushed to her side. Something was terribly wrong. As Vicky hung up the phone, she looked over at me and gasped out between sobs, "That was the Highway Patrol. Cathy has just died in an auto accident, not even a mile from work."

There are no words in any language to describe how I felt. I had found the most beautiful and perfect woman on the planet for me. She felt the same about me. She was gone; and I was destroyed.

My blue merle Australian Shepard, Pepper, saw the tears streaming down my face and jumped into my lap. She buried her head hard against mine as if she felt my pain and loss. I was speechless. Everyone in the house had tears in their eyes, and I needed to get away.

Pepper and I headed out the front door and walked up and down the quiet neighborhood streets until well after midnight as tears continued to flow from my eyes. I didn't want to live any more. I felt I had no reason to go on.

Over the next two weeks I spoke very little. I couldn't even have a conversation with anyone. I went to work building homes everyday, but I was obviously quieter than normal. My boss even told me that I should take a couple of weeks off, although he needed me on the job sites. After work, I would just go to my room or go for a walk. I didn't eat much, and I didn't even want to surf. There was no use drowning my sorrow in alcohol or drugs; it would serve no purpose. Friends urged me to go surfing, but I always declined even though it was something I had usually done almost daily.

On the weekend mornings, Pepper and I would walk all the way to the beaches of Montana De Oro State Park, well over five miles round trip. I was well known in the town. I was a surfboard shaper, a respected builder, and a hard-core big wave rider. People driving along the road would stop to ask me how I was or if I needed a ride, but my responses were minimal. I was depressed, hurt, and sad. I felt like I was dead. Friends tried to cheer me up, but I could only walk away without saying a word.

Late one night, about a month after Cathy's death, I could tell the surf was huge by the thundering sounds of rolling waves in the still night air. The next morning I was up before dawn. I put my wetsuit and surfboard in the back of the truck and Pepper jumped into the cab. I drove out to a surf spot near the end of the state park that we called "Screamers."

Through the pre-dawn darkness, my dog and I walked down the path about a quarter mile to the beach. As the sun started to rise, I could see perfect sets of sixteen- to twenty-foot waves breaking right in front of the jagged rocks that gave the spot its name. I put on my wetsuit and booties. I took the leash off my board. A surfboard's leash is sometimes a surfer's only lifeline in dangerous surf conditions. I told my dog that I loved her and kissed her forehead. The look in Pepper's eyes was one of sadness, as if she knew my intentions. I wasn't planning on coming back, and my body would probably never be found in surf like this.

I hit the water paddling hard. I was going to surf some insane, huge waves before I died. It would be the perfect ending for me. As I reached the takeoff point out beyond the jagged, jetty-like rock formations, I saw continuous huge sets of waves marching in. I pivoted my board towards shore and shouted, "I love you, Cathy!" as I paddled into my first wave. It was about two stories high. My takeoff was late, and I free fell airborne for the top third of the wave, pitched towards shore by the thick lip at the crest of the massive wave. As my fins made contact with the wave's face, I set my edge and snapped my bottom turn before reaching the bottom. The lip pitched out way over me, and I was in a tube that was big enough to hold a semi. I was shot out the end of the wave like a cannonball, and as I kicked a turnout at the end, I got about twenty feet of air. I was lucky that my board landed about thirty feet away. I retrieved it quickly and paddled back out.

I caught three more huge waves, each bigger than the one before, and my takeoffs were later each time. I challenged God to show me that I was supposed to survive because I felt I no longer had any reason to live. My tube rides were deeper and deeper. Each time I kicked out of the wave, I got lucky getting to my board before the next wave hit me. I had got my great rides in, and it was time to call it done. On my next wave, I planned to take off right in front of the rocks and make sure I was so late on the takeoff that I would be instant hamburger on the jagged rocks in front of me.

I didn't paddle as hard on this last huge wave. The lip pitched me out in front of it, and I was engulfed in tons of water being pitched right into the rocks. I felt my feet lose contact with my board. This was it. I was being thrown directly into the meat grinder—and I felt at peace in the slow motion silence.

As the enormous volume of water hit the rocks, it created a cushion with its rebound. The water that had already contacted the rocks before me was now like an airborne current of liquid sweeping me clear of direct impact. I ripped my wetsuit on the rocks as I glanced off them. I was tossed around under the water like a rag in a washing machine, bouncing off sharp rocks below the surface.

As I popped up for air, I saw my surfboard shoreward of me, banging against the rocks in the turbulence. I was surprised to see it was still in one piece. The water in the channels was rushing quickly to shore in between the jetty-like rock formations of Screamers. I reached the shoreline quickly in a rush of water similar to the rapids of a fast-moving river. I saw Pepper watching me from the rocks above as she barked loudly. I wasn't happy to be alive, but I wasn't unhappy that I was either. I actually felt kind of neutral as I climbed the rocks.

I noticed that I was bleeding from a few minor lacerations on my arms and legs, and the salt water made the cuts sting a little as the cold fifty-degree temperature of the ocean wore off. I didn't care.

Pepper came running at me and jumped airborne into my arms. She wouldn't stop licking my face after I caught her. I guess she was happy I was alive, and that was good enough for me for the time being. Pepper and I walked back up the hill to the truck and I drove home in my wetsuit, not even thinking about getting into dry clothes. I was indifferent to my near-death experience and only thoughts of Cathy filled my mind.

When we got home, my roommates were loading their surfboards and wetsuits into their trucks. I hopped out of my truck in my wetsuit and when I started taking it off, they saw the rips and tears as well as the blood running down my arms and legs.

One of the guys walked over to my truck and, as he pulled my surfboard out, he shouted, "You crazy PSYCHO! Where did you go? Screamers by yourself? Holy shit! ... look at his board, guys!"

I calmly said, "My board is history. It was time for a new one anyway. It's big out there today. Got a few insane tubes. Got beat up."

"Where's your leash? And why didn't you wake us up to go with you?" one of them asked.

I told them that it must have broken, and a roommate asked, "Then where are the pieces?" They all knew what I had done, but no one felt free to confront me further. (Later that day, that same roommate brought me my surfboard's leash. He told me he had found it just lying on the beach at Screamers, and that he knew what I had done, but wouldn't talk about it with anyone else.)

I said, "Hey, guys, I learned something today. As long as enough water hits the rocks before you do, you're not going to die."

They all smiled and my roommate Jimbo commented, "Hey, good to see you go surfing, bro! BUT NO MORE SCREAMERS ALONE for awhile or we're going to tie you up!"

"Go surfing, guys! Canyon is probably safer," I said as I reached for the garden hose to rinse the blood off my arms and legs.

Recovering from Cathy's death was a slow process. It was months before I felt like myself again. I took it one day at a time. The thought of dating never even crossed my mind for almost a year. I worked, I surfed, I drank beers with the guys, and I played Frisbee with my dog. I shaped and airbrushed some of the best and most artistic surfboards I ever built during this period of my life, and memories of the woman I loved filled my head and heart while I did it. It seemed that my dog and my memories of Cathy were all I needed for the present.

As time passed, I pushed myself harder at work. I could do the work of two carpenters in a day. In the surf, I seemed invincible. I had no fear of death or injury. I even surfed at times when I knew great white sharks were in the water. The carcasses of large sea cows bobbed in the surf with semi-circular missing chunks that were three to four feet in diameter. I didn't care; I went surfing anyway. I would have welcomed death, but not by my own hand. I was prepared to die by destiny.

I tuned up my body and mind daily with a hundred one-arm fingertip pushups for each arm followed by a hundred sit-ups and stretching exercises inspired by martial arts and surfing motions. I viewed work as getting paid to work out. I was in the best physical shape of my life. I felt balanced, but Cathy was missing. I was empty and alone except for a small group of friends and my dog.

I had an older friend named Jim. He was the UPS delivery driver who had delivered the surfboard fins to our factory back in the day. He had retired, then he and his wife had opened a liquor store and deli down by the bay where a lot of construction workers ate lunch every day.

During the summer of 1986, I went in for lunch and there was a new girl working. I had heard some of the guys talking about her on various job sites for about a week. Jim introduced her to me since she was new in town, and that is how I met the woman I eventually married. We dated for a few weeks, and I asked her to move into a house I had rented. A few months later, I asked her to marry me. We went down to the local courthouse and didn't even tell friends or family we were married for almost a year.

My wife was socially outgoing and well-liked. Before we were married, there were occasionally small things that didn't feel right to me—I'd catch her in little white lies or exaggeration used to manipulate others. I passed it off as insignificant—I told myself I was just over-thinking or analyzing too much. No human being is perfect. Most human beings lean toward being self-centered. Some also yearn to be someone they are not, some perhaps driven to this by the conditioning of society, and the programming or experiences that have occurred in their lives.

I knew I could never expect to mesh with any woman the way Cathy and I had. In hindsight, perhaps I married my wife on the rebound. Lonely and fearful that I would never meet another compatible woman, I perhaps closed my eyes to the small but repetitive warning signs. I had lost something so perfectly wonderful, and the psychological need to fill that void existed. Whatever the case, things were good most of the time for the first year or so, but other red flag behaviors began to surface.

For example, my wife wasn't feeling well that first winter we were together, though she didn't discuss it with me. Her normal energy level just seemed off. She had gone to the doctor the week before, but she wouldn't tell me anything about it... not who she saw, what the doctor had to say, or any other information about the appointment for that matter.

One Saturday my friend Jim showed up at the front door in the middle of the day while my wife was at work at his deli.

As I opened the front door, I saw that Jim had a six-pack of imported beers and a plate of food in his arms—and he had tears in his eyes! He entered and set everything on the dining room table.

I quickly asked, "What's wrong, Jim? Is everything ok?" Jim was a big man. Tall and heavyset, he stepped towards me and enveloped me in a bear hug. I felt his tears soaking the shoulder of my t-shirt as I hugged him back. He had never shown emotion like that in all the years I had known him. I thought that perhaps something had happened to his wife or son. We sat down at the small table, and he opened two beers with an opener attached to his keychain as he wiped his face. But he couldn't stop crying and didn't seem to be ashamed to show this deep emotion in front of me. Something was very wrong.

He began in a shaky voice, "I am so sorry for you. How come these things happen to one of the best people I have ever met? Why you? You love and care for everybody. You put everybody before yourself. Everyone I know looks up to you! And ..."

His head went down on the table, and he cried even harder as I stood and put my hand on his shoulder saying, "Tell me what's going on; I want to help you. I have never seen you like this!"

He raised his head and wiped his tears again, saying, "A year and a half ago, you lost Cathy. It destroyed you. I didn't know if my friend would ever come back to us, but you did, you made it back. Everybody loves you. Now you have the life you deserve, and your wife is dying from cancer..."

"WHAT?" I asked loudly. "Who told you this? I don't know anything about this!"

He appeared shocked that I didn't know as he said, "She did. Her mother has leukemia, and it runs in the family."

"I know her mother has had leukemia, but I was under the impression that it was in remission. I haven't met my in-laws yet. They live in Ukiah, up north," I said. "Don't you think that if my wife had cancer, I would know at least something about it? I know she has been feeling low on energy for the last couple of weeks, but if a doctor has diagnosed her with cancer, the doctor would be obligated to inform her husband, don't you think?"

Jim's expression changed as he realized that I honestly believed my wife didn't have cancer and that he and his wife were being manipulated. He stopped crying and said, "This is embarrassing now; I'm so sorry."

"You have no reason to be sorry. I'm going to get to the bottom of this when she walks in the door! Jim, little stuff similar to this has been happening for some time now. I keep passing it off. If she does have cancer and I am wrong, then I am a piece of shit—but I am pretty sure that's not the case. Is this why she sometimes comes home with a bottle of wine and food from work saying, 'Jim and Jenny insisted I bring this home'?"

Jim had a serious look on his face as I said, "If I am right, then I owe you and everybody else she has been telling this to an apology!"

He replied with, "Do you really think she would do such a thing?"

"I'm sorry to say that I am starting to see a pattern. Let's just put this conversation on hold until I can establish the truth. I am not a doctor, Jim, but I know a lot of shit. Symptoms of most cancers creep up on people. They don't happen overnight to most. A doctor is not going to diagnose cancer during one visit. Let's split this sandwich you brought over and have a beer—and let's talk about something else."

Jim took a deep breath and said, "Yeah, I made this sandwich for you, and we just got these beers in stock." He smiled and continued, "You know, I meant all the things I said about you. We clicked the first day I brought those packages to your surfboard factory. You are a great friend, and no matter what happens in life, my wife and I will always be your friends."

I thanked him and he said, "When you and Cathy used to come into our store, my wife and I were so happy for both of you. My wife used to say, 'Your friend is such a nice guy. Those two are a perfect match. What a lucky couple.' I told her that you were the one that helped me solidify my decision to buy the liquor store and that I used to hang out at the surfboard factory and chat with you every time I had a delivery ... Hey, I hope you don't mind me bringing up the subject of Cathy?"

"No, Jim, I'm fine with it. Between you and me, I still miss her and probably always will," I said. We then talked about how construction work seemed to be slowing down and which local contractors were keeping busy. Jim always had his eyes on the bigger picture of the local economy.

When my wife got home around dusk, I confronted her with, "How are you feeling today, Honey?"

She said she felt fine, so I said, "Anything wrong that I should know about? What happened at your doctor visit last week? In fact, where is the paperwork from your visit? I want to know what the doctor said."

She replied, "That's private."

"Private? My wife doesn't think her husband should know she's dying of cancer while she tells everyone else in town that she is?"

She instantly went pale and stormed away from me to the bedroom. I lingered for a couple of minutes then entered the bedroom. "You need to tell me what's going on."

It took quite awhile for her story to come out. She told me that she found out she was pregnant, had a miscarriage and had to have a D&C. She said she didn't want to upset me and was fine now.

All this did was make me feel more distant from her. Why wouldn't she tell me about this? Was she even pregnant by me? What was really going on? I acted as if her answer was both believed and accepted, but she was destroying any trust I had for her. In time, everything went back to normal ... well—almost normal.

I talked to Jim about two weeks later and he said there were some suspicious things going on at their store. He had recently hired another girl to work the deli and cash register, and product had been missing lately. In addition, the register was coming up short almost daily. I told him that bottles of wine or food hadn't been showing up at our house. Jim told me that he had secretly had some video security installed in the store because the missing inventory was starting to add up quickly. He and his wife were having to work more shifts in order to keep an eye on things. About two months later, Jim informed me that he had to fire both my wife and the other girl. They were both taking things, but none of it ever reached our home.

In 1986-87, building construction had slowed down in San Luis Obispo County due to water shortages. Work became sparse. My wife was about five months pregnant with our son, and things were alright at home.

A friend, in fact a roommate from before I was married, was running a big job down in the canyons above Beverly Hills and he called me one day to ask me to work on his crew. He was rebuilding a huge home for a very famous actor, so I took the job, working as a lead carpenter for a fairly large construction company based out of Agoura, California, just west of Los Angeles and inland from Malibu. This required a lot of driving in my old beat up Toyota truck.

Almost every client we did work for was a celebrity in the motion picture industry or someone of notable standing. I was making excellent wages, which offset the long weekly commute. I would often put in over fifty-hour work weeks to keep the jobs ahead of schedule. Our company had a reputation of always completing jobs before projected deadlines while doing the highest quality work.

Within a couple of months, I had been promoted to project manager by the general contractor to run a half-million dollar kitchen remodel for a famous producer in the middle of Beverly Hills. Up until then, I was a lead carpenter working under my friend, Rob. Our company had a crew of over two dozen very talented builders. The celebrity whose home I was currently working on was upset that I was being transferred from his job to start another project.

My wife and I continued to reside 250 miles north on the Central Coast instead of relocating down to southern California. I would usually spend the weekday nights at my family's home in Ventura County while I worked out the week in Beverly Hills or Malibu.

In early 1988, the weeks prior to our son's birth, my wife was with me, staying at my parents' home. I had scheduled some time off for the week the doctor predicted our son's arrival, but my wife went into labor during the middle of the last week before her due date. Our son was born in the town I grew up in, and we drove back home to the Central Coast that next weekend.

We were soon settled back on the Central Coast and getting comfortable with the routine of being new parents. Friends were visiting daily to see our new family addition. Everyone was happy—at least, I know I was. I did projects around the house and worked on surfboards in the garage, taking advantage of my time off.

My close surfing friend, Jimbo, was a drywall contractor. Before I took the job down south, we used to surf together almost daily. In fact, Jimbo was one of my roommates from before and he had stopped by in the late evening to tell me the surf was big. He asked my wife if I was "allowed" to go surfing in the morning, and she replied that I needed to go surfing.

Jimbo picked me up at dawn in his Isuzu work truck. Of course, our first surf check would be Screamers in the state park. We ran down the trail as we watched big sets of waves peel perfectly in front of the jagged rocks. Our surf dogs, Pepper and Heineken, chased at our heels, excited to be together at the beach.

Screamers was a dangerous surf spot. We arrived at the spot where we always changed into our wetsuits, but we always watched the waves for awhile first. Swell direction and tidal conditions had to be optimum for the surf break to be safe. Jimbo and I had the reputation of being big wave riders. Most of our friends did too, and most of them rode tri-fin surfboards that I had custom built for them. Although many called us crazy, all our friends were excellent watermen, able to act as lifeguards in the powerful surf if needed. Not many people had the confidence and skill to surf Screamers when it was big. It didn't break unless the waves were at least one and a half times overhead.

I guess I was usually the one to initiate changing into wetsuits, and Jimbo made the comment that I was slow in deciding that day. But there was a little bit of southerly direction in the swell, which was unfavorable. Just then, a two-story wave closed out the whole bay. Waves like that could wash you into the rocks if you were caught off guard. We would just have to be more selective on our wave choices.

I said, "We've surfed this place a lot bigger and a lot more dangerous, but something doesn't feel right. There are perfect barrels peeling in between those south sets."

"You never puss out! You're always first in the water and first to the outside. What's up? We haven't surfed together in weeks! You pussin' out?" Jimbo asked as we both laughed at his ribbing.

"There are great waves between those south sets, but something feels wrong ... you or me puss out? That's the funniest thing I ever heard!"Then I experienced an epiphany and quickly explained, "Jimbo, I know what I am feeling! I'm a dad now ... I have a kid. I just realized that I can't get injured or die out there today. This is really a weird feeling. I never hesitate here! This place has spiritual meaning to me. How about we deal with the crowd at Hazards? It'll be bigger, and the southerly direction in this swell will give us long hollow lefts if the rights are too crowded."

Jimbo replied, "Wow, you are a dad now. You're being responsible, and that's good! Yeah, Canyon will be bigger and we can grab some good rights before the crowds show up. It's big enough to make spectators out of most of them. It'll be mostly locals and the South County crew later on, then we just shift over to the north side of the reef."

We raced our dogs back to his truck and drove a mile back up the road to park. Hazards Canyon was good! Sets were big, double overhead easily. We surfed both sides of the reef, and the crowd wasn't bad at all. There were plenty of good waves to go around. I really needed that day of surfing. We surfed until we could barely paddle anymore. The next two days were big as well. I got my fill of the big surf that I had been missing... something I needed to keep me feeling balanced.

I returned to work two weeks after our son's birth, and my younger brother from Livermore, California, called me on the job site to say he had found me a great deal on an almost new Dodge truck. He worked for Chrysler and could get me a repossessed vehicle at auction price. I rented a car for the family to drive up to the Bay Area on the weekend to buy my new work truck. My brother saved me thousands of dollars, and the truck was like brand new.

My wife, son and I continued driving north after getting the truck and visited her parents in Ukiah. This was the first time I had met them, and they were introduced to their first grandchild. We only stayed overnight because I had to be back to the jobs in Beverly Hills immediately.

The next year and a half were good. My wife was happy and very attentive to our son. We had other friends with young children, and she and my son would sometimes come down to southern California for the work week. One very famous movie star and his wife even invited them to come down to the job site in Malibu to spend the day on their private beach while I was working. The majority of the time, though, my wife and son were on the Central Coast. I was home only on weekends or while our construction company was in between jobs. Needless to say, as time progressed and our son got older, this put an incredible strain on our marriage. Well, that may not be the best way to phrase that. It might be more accurate to say that my time away from home gave my wife the ability to party her life away, and the situation got worse as time passed. Friends would come over and visit when I was home on weekends. A couple of them, though afraid, told me stories of unsavory things they witnessed my wife doing around town on occasion.

I began to bring the family with me more often, staying at my parents' house for a couple of weeks at a time. This enabled me to spend more time with my young boy and my wife, and I felt that the situation had improved and her behavior patterns had changed.

In the winter of 1989-90, my wife and son were home, up north. One weekday I drove all the way home unexpectedly after work just to surprise my family because I missed them. It took over three hours from Malibu. When I pulled into my driveway, there were about a dozen cars parked in the street near my house. It was almost 10:00 p.m., and there was a huge party with loud music and drugs all over the place. I didn't recognize anyone. As I entered the house, I saw my wife snorting a huge line of cocaine with several people on the couch.

I yelled, "Everybody get the hell out of my house! Cops are on the way!" I rushed to the bedroom, grabbed my son and drove to the beach. I returned home after an hour to find that my home was trashed. Mirrors and glass-framed pictures from the walls had cocaine residue all over them, broken bottles littered the room, etc.

That week, I gave a two-week notice on my job because I felt I had to move back home for my son's sake and to try to save my marriage. In what I considered our first reconciliation, my wife promised that she would change and avoid the crowd of people she hung around with. Once I returned home, I worked for local contractors as much as I could, and she took a job waitressing at a local establishment—but she soon began coming home late after partying at the bar. There were rumors that she even stripped at an after-hours birthday party in exchange for drugs. After that, there were too many incidents over the next several months to even recount. She left me and had a drug dealer boyfriend try to kill me for my million-dollar life insurance policy on one occasion. During one of our separations, she even got pregnant by an eighteen-year-old cocaine dealer and had an abortion, but I didn't find out about this until I had already let her back into my life again.

Life was a literal nightmare. Our relationship became very ugly and culminated in her filing for divorce, claiming that I was violent—then she returned months later, begging me to take her back again. I decided to get rid of almost everything we owned and move up to her parents' home and re-establish work and our living situation. I knew I needed to get her far away from the people she was associating with, and her parents agreed even though they listened to lies she told them about me. I cared about her, but my desire to be with her had faded, and my trust was destroyed. I was disgusted by the countless things that had transpired. I actually felt she was a lost cause, but I was determined to give our marriage one last chance out of concern for our son.

CHAPTER 3

<hr />

DECISION AND DIRECTION

I made the first trip to Ukiah by myself with a rented open trailer and large items for storage. I spent the night at my in-law's and talked to them for hours. Though my wife had promised all of us that she would never go down her current road again, her parents were still willing to let us stay with them for a few months. Their main concern was to have a healthy environment for their only grandson and to help their daughter recover.

I had several trusted friends watching over my wife and son or staying at the house while I was gone. Since I didn't have to worry about them, I took time on the way back home to stop by construction sites to look for work. So much money had disappeared before I quit working down south and separated the bank accounts that the cost of relocating would bankrupt me. The long drive also gave me time to think about my current situation.

While I was home for a few days, I sold all of our extra vehicles. Among them were my '62 Karmann Ghia and '69 Toyota truck, and my wife's '70 Subaru and '78 BMW 320i. I liked to restore and work on cars in my free time, and I always had several projects going to occupy myself.

I made a second trip alone to her parents' house with the truck and trailer packed full, and these items finished filling the rented storage unit on the outskirts of Ukiah. After a brief stop to see my in-laws, I was back on the road to the Central Coast. A few days later, my wife and I said good-bye to our close friends and headed for her parents' home. My wife drove her white Celica with her dog, Aussie riding shotgun. Pepper rode shotgun in my Dakota truck, both vehicles packed full of our remaining possessions and necessities.

Our first few weeks were quiet as we acclimated to the new surroundings. Our son was happy to spend time with his maternal grandparents, and they were happy to have us. Their daughter seemed to be happy and balanced, but bored.

Despite freezing temperatures, I would jog most mornings before breakfast. After breakfast, I would split wood with my retired father-in-law and talk. He was not actually my wife's biological father, and this was a second marriage for him. Stout and well built, he fit the picture of a "mountain man." My wife's mother, on the other hand, was a thin woman. She and my wife hadn't been on good terms for years prior to our move to Ukiah. Her mom was intelligent and outspoken, and formerly employed by a California governor. I liked both of my wife's parents, but her mother was definitely headstrong. She had a tough life, raising a couple of children from different fathers. She also had leukemia, but it had gone into remission at some point after I first met her when we introduced her to her first grandchild.

Every other day I would spend the entire day driving within a sixty-mile radius, checking out job sites. Construction work was minimal compared to the number of opportunities in more populated areas. On occasion, I would stop into local bars and have a beer to strike up conversations with the locals and the bartender to find out about construction sites. I would always get leads, but projects were very small and worked by tight-knit local crews. No one was hiring.

One day, over two months after we had arrived, I ran across a large condominium complex. There were over 150 concrete slabs complete and ready for framing. All the underground utilities were laid and covered. The main streets were paved and the curb, gutter, and sidewalks were formed up. They looked ready to pour concrete. To me, this looked like a good year or more of work for a large construction crew. I saw the door of the job trailer ajar, so I parked my truck and walked in.

One of four men inside asked, "Can I help you?" Another man offered me a Styrofoam cup of fresh coffee.

I said, "Good morning, gentlemen, is one of you the project superintendent? I have just moved up from central and southern California, and I am looking for a good company to work for."

"Well, what can you do?" asked the tallest man.

"Well, sir, I have been a project manager, building homes for famous celebrities in the greater Los Angeles area for the last couple of years. I do every trade of residential construction," I replied.

"Sure you do!" quipped a shorter man in a tone that challenged me to prove it.

In an upbeat tone I offered, "Let me go get my briefcase out of my truck and show you some of my work; I'll be right back."

The shorter man who had pushed me to prove my words followed me to the door and turned back to the others saying, "Hey, guys, get over here. Check out this guy's truck. He might not be bullshitting us."

I returned with a smile, carrying my briefcase and a magazine. As I sat my briefcase on one of the desks, I handed the magazine to the shorter man. He looked at the cover to see that it was from earlier that year, April 1990. He read the title out loud to his friends, "Better Homes and Gardens Architect Edition," then asked, "What's this for?"

I said, "Flip to the dog-eared page. That's the kitchen I did for the producer of an extremely popular Hollywood game show."

Everyone set down their coffee cups and gathered around. I showed them assorted job logs, projected work schedules, and dozens of Polaroid pictures of our work. They also viewed letters or notes from clients that thanked me and wished me well. They all recognized the movie stars' names.

The tallest man spoke, "I own one quarter of this company. If this project weren't shut down right now, I would hire you on the spot and retire. We are a big company, and we need a guy like you! Heck, I could just sit back and let you run the show."

"Why is the project shut down?" I asked.

"This Gulf War crap has our investors paranoid about the economy. I don't see anything happening for six to eight months, at least. Leave me your number and contact information; I'll be happy to call you as we find out more in say, six months."

I handed him one of my old business cards with my changed phone number handwritten on it. They all wanted me to tell some stories, so I ended up in their office until almost noon. They offered to buy me lunch and a beer in town, but I told them I had better keep pounding the pavement for work. One fellow wrote down the addresses of about six other construction projects for me, but they all commented that everything they knew of locally was also shut down due to the Gulf War and economy.

I returned home, a little depressed that construction work was going to be near impossible to find. I got the classified section of the newspaper from my mother-in-law and began calling on any kind of job over the next few days. I even tried to get hired delivering pizzas, but telephone calls were cut short when they realized or stated that I was way over-qualified. There was no point extending my job-hunting radius since I had called larger construction firms all the way down in Santa Rosa, California, which was about a two-and-a-half hour drive each way.

My mother-in-law began to comment day in and day out because I hadn't found work yet. I'd never had trouble finding work in more densely populated areas. The stress of being ridden continuously was starting to really bother me, but I held my tongue. She would accost me accusingly about trivial things like my wife bringing her dog in the house at night—which wasn't allowed, but also which I wasn't even aware of my wife doing.

I began to regret moving to Ukiah. I figured I probably should have accepted the offer from my last big job for a salaried partnership in company ownership. It would also have been better if I had moved my family down to southern California instead of here to Ukiah. December arrived, and I still had no job. My wife had looked for waitressing jobs, but once again there weren't as many openings or establishments as in other areas. I continued to check the newspaper daily for work—and that's when it happened. I saw an ad seeking people with a background in computers and electronics. I had seen the ads before, but figured they were probably for recruiting military personnel for the Gulf War because of the way they were worded. I decided to make the call.

The man who answered told me these jobs were for the Navy. He said I sounded too old and asked my age. He told me that I could enlist up to the age of thirty-four and that he could have someone call me in the next couple of days.

I said, "Rather than wait for a call, couldn't I expedite things by calling a recruiting office? Where is the closest one to Ukiah, California? Can you connect me?" He connected me directly to the Santa Rosa office, and the recruiter there asked me to drive down the next day to talk to him.

The following afternoon, my wife and son travelled to Santa Rosa with me just after lunch. We all needed a break from the tension at her parents' house. The drive was nice, and we had an early dinner at a fast food establishment before going to the recruiting office. There were three younger men on duty when we arrived, and the one in charge was eager to talk to me. The others occupied my wife and son as I filled out questionnaires while they did extensive background checks. They gave me a short pre-ASVAP test, and one of them started talking about the real test, including its background and history. I told him that he didn't need to elaborate. I had learned all about the hardest test ever designed during psychology classes in high school and college.

College credits from my transcripts prompted them to tell me that I would qualify for a fast track through officer's training after my first "A" school. They told me that their computer system determined that my skills and abilities indicated Fire Control to be my best job choice.

My wife asked, "What's so good about being a fireman?" They explained that Fire Control was related to weapons systems. One of the recruiters began to elaborate on the duties of the job and noted that one had to be in the top ten percent to get that job assignment.

By the end of our meeting, the recruiters had asked me to show up with my family no later than 3:30 the next afternoon so the Navy could buy us all dinner at a nice Mexican restaurant down just a few doors from the office. From there I would say good-bye to my family and be transported to MEPS (Military Entrance Processing Station)

Headquarters in Oakland to take the entrance exam and go through the induction process. I told them I had to think about it and that I would call them well before noon the next day with my decision.

On the drive back to Ukiah, my wife and I talked at length about everything that would transpire if I decided to join the Navy. We talked about the possibility of being stationed and living abroad, possibly even Hawaii, where we would be very close to my mother's family.

Our son kept saying, "My daddy has built homes for movie stars (as he named the ones he had met), and now he is going to be on a big Navy ship firing missiles at the enemies..." He was excited, but I was unsure. My wife seemed almost indifferent.

CHAPTER 4

SET IN MOTION

The next morning we were all up bright and early. Pancakes were already on the table, and her parents were anxious to hear about the appointment with the Navy recruiters. My mother-in-law knew how hard she was being on me and wanted to know how her daughter's husband was going to support his family and what the plan was. My son kept saying little phrases like, "My daddy is going to shoot down the bad guys. That's what the Navy guys told me." We had to finish breakfast and get him off to the other room to play with his toys so the four of us could have an uninterrupted discussion.

We talked about how long it would be until my wife and son were relocated with me. We talked about the possibility of being stationed in Hawaii or a foreign country and how that experience would benefit our whole family. I made it clear that my salary would not be big and that the real opportunities would come after my six-year enlistment—and there at the table that morning, I made the decision to join.

I called the recruiting office to inform them of my decision. We left Ukiah around 1:00 in the afternoon. It was a nice winter day as we drove the two and a half hours to Santa Rosa. Traffic was light, and I was driving five to ten miles over the speed limit the whole way. Everyone seemed to be in good spirits.

The three recruiters were waiting when we arrived at the Santa Rosa recruiting office right on schedule. They locked the office doors, and the six of us walked down to the Mexican restaurant. They had made reservations, and a big table was waiting for us in the impressively decorated restaurant. The guys told us to order anything we wanted, telling us that the Navy was picking up the bill. When one of them asked our nearly three-year-old son what he wanted, he replied quickly.

"I want a taco and a burrito and an enchilada and more chips and salsa. Can I have a soda, Mommy? Oh, what does that man have? I want one of those too!"

My wife replied, "Your eyes are bigger than your tummy. I think they must have children's portions, and you can try some of Mommy's and Daddy's food if you are still hungry." The ranking recruiter said, "He can order an adult meal. He's a growing boy and will grow up big and strong like his father," as he looked at me and smiled.

I remarked, "Well, okay, son. I think these guys are trying to pre-recruit you," as everyone laughed.

The waitress returned and took all of our orders. She asked me what I wanted to drink.

I asked, "Gentlemen, would it be okay if I had a Corona or Pacifico?"

The head recruiter replied with, "Well, you have about four hours before your test, so yeah, we were planning on ordering some beers. Miss, let us have a pitcher of Bud Lite."

"I hate Bud Lite, but I won't be picky since the Navy is buying. Doesn't Bud give you guys a headache? Oh, and one pitcher is not even going to fill all our glasses once."

The waitress said, "He's right, how about I start you all off with two? I'll be right back."

When she returned, she poured glasses for the four of us, emptying the first pitcher and setting the second in the middle of the table. My wife drank iced tea and our son had his soda.

We munched on chips and salsa as we waited for our meals. All three men had stories to tell of their travels and tours of duty for the Navy. My wife was very interested in hearing about the Mediterranean, Indonesia, the Philippines, Japan, and Hawaii. We were all enjoying their tales, occasionally topping off our beer glasses.

Our food arrived and the meals were quite a bit larger than I expected. There was no way my son would make even a dent in the food he had ordered. The waitress put a fresh pitcher of beer in the center of the table and filled my glass with the end of the second pitcher's contents. Conversation continued as we ate. Our food was great, and my son actually finished most of his meal. The recruiters told us that not every enlistee got this kind of treatment, but they really liked our whole family.

After dinner, I could tell a couple of the guys were starting to get a little bit buzzed from the beers. I filled my glass again and topped off the glass of the man to my right, emptying the third pitcher. The man to my left signaled the waitress, and she brought a fourth pitcher of Bud Lite.

Some of the stories the men told were really funny. Everyone was involved in the conversation, even our son. I sat across the table from my wife and child, with two men to my right and one to my left. The man next to my wife started telling a story about being on leave in the Philippines and what had happened in a brothel with the Military Police being called in. The recruiter next to me kicked his shin hard under the table because the story was not appropriate for my wife and child. My wife laughed as the man sitting next to her loudly exclaimed, "OUCH!"

The fourth pitcher of beer emptied as stories continued, and the ranking recruiter decided we had better cut off the beer. When he poured the last of the pitcher into my glass, it wasn't much more than two sips so he said, "Okay, one more," as he motioned to the waitress who wasn't far from our table.

The man to my right excused himself from the table to go to the restroom. Everyone was talking about how great the food was when the waitress returned. She poured my glass to the top, and the man next to me motioned for her to stop when his glass was half full.

As the recruiter who had gone to the bathroom returned, he stopped for a second. He realized that he was pretty buzzed. He motioned the other men to come over to him, so they excused themselves and met their friend a few feet from our table. They were close enough for me to overhear their conversation. I poured another beer for myself as all three men talked.

"I think we fucked up, guys. I can't drive right now," lamented the first recruiter.

"He has to take the ASVAP in a couple of hours. None of us is okay to drive. We could go to the brig for this. If he is drunk when he takes that test or doesn't get a good score, we could be in a world of shit," bemoaned the second man.

The head recruiter then said, "Okay, this is what we do. You go back to the office and call someone in to drive. We have to leave in the next thirty minutes. We need to start drinking coffee."

Two of the men returned to the table, sitting on each side of me. The waitress came over to clear the table as we talked. The waitress went to refill my near-empty glass, but the man to my right motioned her to stop.

I said, "Wait a minute here. I overheard your conversation. You guys might be a little buzzed, but I am fine. I can drive us all down to Oakland. Do you want to give me a sobriety test right now? How about the alphabet backwards? ZYXWVUTSRQPONMLKJIHGFEDCBA!"

Everyone was stunned. People at other tables looked our way as I quickly rattled off the alphabet backwards, loud and clear. The waitress smiled and filled my glass, remarking with a laugh that she didn't know anyone who could do that sober.

My wife chipped in, "My husband's fine. It would take a couple more pitchers for him to even start to get drunk," as she laughed before giving the waitress a dirty look for what she perceived as the woman being flirtatious with me.

I finished the last pitcher of beer by myself as the guys paid the bill and tip. They showed me the credit card which had "UNITED STATES NAVY" embossed as the name of the cardholder.

We walked out to the curb and awaited the arrival of our transportation. When the dark blue Ford minivan pulled up, I hugged and kissed my wife and child as we said our good-byes. I told my wife to drive safely back to Ukiah and that I would call before I shipped out the next day.

The drive to the base located in Oakland would take a couple of hours. The driver, who had not yet met me, was lecturing all of us about drinking at dinner and all the things that could happen if someone found out. He passed around a pack of chewing gum and recommended that we all stop for coffee.

The driver did not know me, so I said, "I am not drunk. While I respect what you have to say, I think you are being a little harsh on your associates here. Thank you for coming in and driving us down, but if I have to listen to you continue this tone and attitude towards everyone in this van for two hours, you can pull over and drop me off on the side of the road. Then you can explain to your superiors why I decided not to enlist."

The two recruiters from Santa Rosa were a little bit shocked at what I said to the driver and one asked, "Is this guy officer material or what?" Everyone in the van laughed.

The conversation changed back to stories of deployment and shore leave in different countries, and this time they included the tales that were not appropriate in front of my wife and son. The driver was just as personable as the other guys, and he had his own stories. We all got along fine, and the drive passed quickly as the sun was setting.

CHAPTER 5

The Written Exam

The Aerostar minivan pulled up to the curb. We had arrived at the Military Entrance Processing Station in Oakland, California. The test was scheduled to start in about twenty-five minutes. The driver reminded the two recruiters escorting me, "Make sure you guys don't breathe on anyone; just drop him off and get back here." He wished me good luck, and one of the other recruiters told the driver to quit being so paranoid.

As I stepped out of the vehicle, my eyes followed a wide set of concrete steps leading almost twenty feet above street level to a tall, older office building. The sun had already dropped well below the horizon. Against the night sky I saw that the building was at least sixteen stories high. The large glass windows lining the front of the first floor were blacked out, emitting no light. The centered, double entry doors were wide open, and a huge beam of bright white fluorescent light spilled out into the night. My thoughts flashed to the positive psychological impact this might have on new enlistees who might be having second thoughts about joining the armed forces. The street lights provided plenty of illumination as we climbed the stairs.

A young man ran out the door of the building with two Military Policemen giving chase. The guards were yelling, "HALT" and "GET BACK HERE!"

My recruiters began telling me how a lot of guys are given the option to join the armed forces as an alternative to jail time, in order to better their lives. They told me the scene we were witnessing was common. A person trying to escape after making the choice to enlist happened almost daily. By the time they were done talking, the fleeing young man was in custody.

As we entered the lobby of the facility, guards were posted at every passageway. My escorts handed my paperwork to a clerk who informed me where I would be taking the exam. My recruiters shook my hand as they wished me good luck and one said, "Call us when you arrive at 'A' school in Chicago. Remember, Fire Control is the job you want; don't let them talk you into something else."

The other encouraged, "Do good on the test! That's your future! Good luck, buddy."

Down a hallway to the left, I saw a gathering group of enlistees as I walked. I approached two very young men closest my path. I greeted them with "How are you guys doing?"

We exchanged handshakes and introductions. I asked them if they were ready for this test. One remarked, "I didn't know what to study; what's on this test?" His comment snagged the attention of a group of four girls and two guys standing about ten feet away. They were all very young, perhaps eighteen to twenty years old.

Their whole group began to walk toward us as they explained in reply, "You can't study for this test because everything you could ever think of could be on it." I elaborated on how there would be questions designed to slow you down and a few questions without correct answers in the choices. I told them that the best advice was to move on if they became frustrated or didn't know the answer to a question and come back to it later.

One young girl, a brunette with glasses who was leading the group of six, smilingly greeted us. I noticed the young women looking down at my left hand. I thought that my age and wedding ring made them feel comfortable to approach the three of us. There were now nine of us gathered together, discussing the upcoming test. There must have been well over three dozen enlistees standing in the hallway, patiently waiting to take that entrance exam.

One of the guys looked at me and said, "It sounds like you know a lot about this test. What is it? What can we expect?" I replied, "The

Military Entrance Exam is called the ASVAP. It is renowned for being the hardest IQ test ever designed. No one can know everything on the test, and no one has ever finished or achieved a perfect score on it. It's impossible."

I looked at the brunette and she started talking about what she knew about the exam, "The ASVAP was designed by dozens of people with IQs higher than Albert Einstein's. The name of it is an acronym that stands for Aptitude, Scholastic, Vocational and Psychological. It even indirectly measures your psychological disposition. How well you do on the test determines the jobs you are qualified for..." I was amazed as she continued on and on, answering questions from everyone. I was impressed by her education and how outgoing she was socially.

She took center stage, and I was relieved. I listened to everything she said and just nodded my head in approval occasionally. I didn't want to be seen as the older "know it all" guy by all the younger recruits. I could tell many in our conversation group were overly nervous about taking the test. Some of the recruits had input to share on how they would take the test, and they urged the others to relax.

Our group broke into smaller conversations, and I asked the brunette if she was joining the armed forces for the educational benefits. She told me that her family couldn't afford to send her to college and medical school. Enlisting in the military was a decision she had made a couple of years earlier. She was fresh out of high school and lived somewhere east of San Francisco.

She asked, "Aren't you a little old to enlist?"

I told her that I was surprised to learn that one could enlist up to the age of thirty-four. I briefly told her about being out of work for a few months and how I was burned out on construction.

The door of our exam room opened and a man in uniform stepped into the corridor saying, "It's time, people. Take a seat and stow all your personal belongings below it. There are no calculators or slide rules allowed. The test is in timed sections." As we all took seats in the classroom-style desks, he continued spelling out all the rules for the exam. He made points about coloring in the bubbles completely and that going back to a section to work on it after the time ran out would result in disqualification. Cheating meant court martial, etc.

Before the test started, I made eye contact with most of the people that were in our group before the test. Most smiled, and a couple of guys looked worried. One cute blonde girl stuck her tongue out and made a funny face at the rest of us to try to get us to laugh. I seem to recall the test administrator sticking out his tongue at her to help relieve some of the tension as some of us quietly laughed.

He smiled after that and began walking down rows to distribute the test booklets individually. I considered that the tests were not all the same. The pencils, scratch paper, and answer cards were distributed to the first person in the row of desks and handed back. We were told that the only reason we could get out of our seat was to sharpen a pencil. We would get a fifteen-minute break about halfway through. There would be no talking allowed during this break, and we would be required to stay within view of guards and officials.

The test was about to start, and I was thinking about the conversation on the drive from Santa Rosa to Oakland, and how I drank five pitchers of beer at dinner with my recruiters. I was not the least bit drunk. I felt relaxed. The test administrator picked up a stopwatch from the desk and told us how much time we were allowed for the first section. I made a mental note of the hands on the wall clock just as he said, "Begin."

The sound of test booklets simultaneously opening filled the room, instantly followed by complete silence. I took a deep breath and started reading and looking at pictures. The first page or two was pattern recognition, progressing images, polygons, circles, and ellipses. Next came pictures of lines and shapes where estimation of length by eye went from full numbers to fractional measurements. Units then switched from common inches to decimal increments and then the metric system.

Next came general knowledge—things like the distance from Earth to Sun, Moon to Earth, and radius of the Earth. The test continued with astronomical units, parsecs, closest stars, and constellations. Questions about our galaxy's shape, estimated size, age, and number of stars soon changed to Earth's tilt, seasons and tides, longitude and latitude.

From there, the test contained questions on geography, cultures, anthropology, archaeology and even evolution. It included magnetic fields, atmospheric conditions, pressures associated with altitude both above and below sea level. Everything and anything you could think of was on this test. This first section was about a third or more of the booklet, almost half of the more than three-hour exam.

Filling in the bubbles of the computer card answer sheet became natural and automatic to me. The sharp pencil was now nicely rounded as I spun it in my hand while reading questions.

The multiple choice format of the test was easier. I could eliminate a couple choices at first glance. When I had to think more deeply on a question, I would make sure all my previous bubbles were filled in completely. The first thing that came to mind was my choice for my answers. I moved fast, taking no time to second guess because I didn't want to waste any time. Every second counted.

The test was made more difficult by the way some answers were worded. For example, some answer sets included "all the above, none of the above, the correct answer is not present, there is no answer," and of course "A and B, all but D," etc. This required reading the answer choices very carefully before choosing.

Questions on the human body followed next—organs, circulatory system, lymph system, nervous system, brain, and synapses. Questions about muscle and skeletal structure were included. There were questions on the animal and plant kingdoms and divisions down to genus-species. Through my head ran "Kingdom-Phylum-Class-Order-Family-Genus-Species," remembered from high school biology and junior high science classes. From there, the test covered psychology, sociology, governments, and countries.

I thought the test followed somewhat of a path, with one group of questions being logically tied to the previous and the next. During the marine biology and oceanographic section I jokingly asked myself, "When are they going to ask the percentage of dolphin meat in a can of tuna?"

Back in the first half of that test section, I had answered the questions on entropy and physics principals. I remembered my high school physics and chemistry teacher, Mr. Don Miller, once saying to the class, "Pay attention, people! Questions about entropy will be on every IQ test you ever take."

Many of the science-related questions were very deep— they addressed atomic structure, polarities, valence electrons, electron shell configuration, chemical combinations, Latin suffixes of "-ate, -ide and –ite,"; acids, bases, litmus testing, and solutions.

Avogadro's Number Value instantly popped into my head when the chemistry section asked about molar concentrations. So did principals of buoyancy and fluids by Bernoulli. Distillation, combustion, and oxidation principals were covered.

Questions on radiation, radioactive decay and energy waves moved toward audio and light wave principals, including focal length of lenses. During this section I remembered my father teaching me (before I was twelve years old) that LASER was an acronym for *Light Amplification through Stimulated Emission of Radiation.* Next came electrical and electronic principals, and quite a few questions on resistance, transistors and circuitry were on the test. These went smoothly. I had studied electrical and electronic engineering in college. I had also taken several electronics classes in high school.

Time passed quickly as I tried to go as fast as I could color in the bubbles. I got to the last page of the section, and I was relieved. When I looked at the wall clock as I set down my pencil, I still had about twenty minutes. So, I went back to the beginning and skimmed over all the questions I wasn't a hundred percent sure of. I had left a couple of the questions blank. As the buzzer went off, the sound of exhales and whispered profanities could be heard from all around the room.

The next section was English, literature, and comprehension. It was much shorter, but I felt it was my weakest section. I glanced at questions before I read the text. I felt this made it easier for me because locating a written passage to answer a question went faster. I was worried about word definitions. Most of the words I wasn't sure of had enough contextual clues to help me solidify my answer. Questions on literary works were fairly general, and the books were well known; but I was still glad when that section was done. I was only a couple of minutes ahead of the clock this time.

We were given our intermission. Straight to the water fountain I went, feeling dehydrated from the beers at dinner. I went to the bathroom to splash water in my face. There were even guards in the restrooms to insure that recruits did not talk about the test.

One enlistee in the bathroom said, "That test is insane!"

The guard present immediately reprimanded him with, "One more word, and you are out. Follow orders!"

I walked out into the hallway and leaned my back against the wall near the door. My eyes met those of the four girls coming out of the ladies' restroom. The blonde who had made the funny face at everyone looked at me. She closed her eyes and tilted her head to her shoulder signifying that she was tired. Another young blonde girl tapped her arm and nodded her head up and down in agreement. The brunette rolled her eyes upward and shook her head side to side.

My response to them was to rub my eyes with both hands, then having my eyes crossed when I removed my hands. The girls tried to suppress their giggles and two guys standing between us in the hall laughed lightly. The guard nearest me gave me a stern look, but he didn't say anything.

The test administrator stepped through the doorway and said, "Break is over." We all returned to our desks and sat down in silence. Someone yawned and a chain reaction went through many of the enlistees, including me.

Science, math, physics, and chemistry word problems and equations were on the next test section. As I recall, we had a little over an hour for this section. I thought this would be the hardest section for everyone.

Basic arithmetic was nowhere to be seen. The test jumped right into analytic geometry and advanced algebra. My memory pulled up equations for circles, spheres, ellipses, hyperbolas, and the like.

Graph plotting and graph-based solutions were also covered. Factoring quadratic equations refreshed in my head quickly.

I had very little work on my scratch paper. I was doing most rough calculations in my head, approximating answers with their correct units of measurement. I mainly used my scratch paper to write down electrical, rotational kinematic, non-factorable quadratic, trigonometric equations and identities from my memory when I needed them.

As I did the trigonometric section, I flashed on the questions in the first test section that dealt with the error that Einstein made in his proof of his famous equation. He had used a trigonometric identity which equaled zero in the denominator, making his equation undefined at that point of his proof. Interpolation equations took little time.

Physics and mathematics problems that might take me fifteen to thirty minutes each were rushed through by rounding up and down to estimate the answer. When provided answers were too close to each other, there was no choice but to do the precise mathematical work longhand for the correct answer. I could do some long physics problems fast as canceling out units enabled me to see the answer's format quickly or at least eliminate all the answers with incorrect units.

I opted for doing everything that went fast first, then returned to all the ones that would take more than ten minutes. This way, if time ran out, I would have more answers complete rather than burning up my time on just a few problems. Calculus-related problems took longer. While derivatives and integrals went relatively fast, limits of functions, summations, logarithm tables and natural logs took me longer.

Balancing chemical equations was just an offshoot of algebra. Pressure and volume problems required remembering basic formulas again. The electrical/electronic problems went relatively fast. The computer science, electrical and electronic engineering courses I had taken for about two years at Cal Poly, San Luis Obispo, made these questions fairly easy.

I had reached the end of that section at about halfway through the time period. I then returned to the almost twenty problems that would take considerably more time. Among those, I was able to find two more that I felt did not have an answer present. One question's answer was not in the correct units, although the numerical value was exact. I had two questions that I had left blank back in the first test section. I completed solving my final problem on this test section.

As I reviewed the two questions I had left blank, the buzzer rang and pencils dropped again.

The next section was coding. At the top of the first page was a long list of five- to six-digit numbers associated with words. Nouns like doctor, nurse, ambulance, and fireman were in the first half of the list or "key."

Some numbers had repositioned digits. For example, nurse might have been 43658, while fireman was 48653, and firetruck was 68435. The word fire was also there. Similarity of words or numbers were there to distract and confuse you. It was harder once I turned the page and had to flip back to the key. I began to identify the number string as another word for the noun, as if it were like another language. Just as I felt I had those codes down, there was a new key and a set of 100 questions. Then came another new code key and its questions. The hardest part was number-letter combinations toward the end.

I colored in bubbles as fast as I could. I was eighty percent done filling the last bubble of my answer card when the buzzer sounded. That section of the test made me perspire a bit, and I wiped my forehead with the forearm of my long-sleeved t-shirt.

One section left, around forty more minutes, and we would be done. This last section was called "mechanical." I didn't know what to expect.

As the test started, I opened the booklet and the mechanical drawings filled the page. They were fairly complex with dozens of gears, side by side and stacked.

I looked at the first question: "If gear 2 rotates clockwise, which direction is gear 134 turning?" I went through this section with relative ease and speed. "If Valve B is in the open position, which direction is the fluid flowing in Tube A?"

Everything in this section was obvious and logical to me. This part was easy because of all my experience working on cars and boats. I often repaired tape decks and electrical equipment, including power tools. Mechanical equipment, assembly, and repair were like an innate ability to me.

I remember the last question of my ASVAP test very well:

The mechanical drawings on the preceding pages depict:
A. a motor
B. a differential
C. a transmission
D. an engine
E. None of the above

I was done extremely early; half the time allotted for that section remained. I looked over the drawings and questions, but had no interest in them. I felt I had scored a hundred percent on the last section. I closed my test booklet and made sure all bubbles were filled in. I stared at the four that I had left blank, unanswered, on the computer card and wrote their numbers down on my scratch paper so that I could review them. I used the pencil's eraser to remove marks outside the bubbles.

I had about twenty minutes to kill. I did not want to turn in my test first or disturb the others taking the test. Being done so early might distract the other enlistees and possibly increase frustration or decrease concentration. I dusted the eraser debris from my answer card. I placed it at the top front of my desk with the pencil laid diagonally on top of it.

The test administrator noticed my actions. We made eye contact, and I lifted the upper corner of my test booklet, as if asking if it was alright to look through the test booklet. He made no gesture or expression to confirm or deny. As I opened the booklet, he paid no attention. I simply looked at the four questions I had left blank to convince myself I made the right choices. I felt my best choice was to leave these four answers blank.

A young man turned in his test fifteen minutes later. Some recruits were distracted as he walked up to the front desk. At two minutes remaining, I turned in my answer card, my scratch paper, pencil, and test booklet. The test administrator smiled at me and picked up my card to look at it. He returned it to the desk and nodded in approval. I was finally done. I returned to my seat as the buzzer rang.

Upon exiting, I lingered in the hall and waited for the majority of our pre-test group to come out. The guys were all pretty quiet, but the girls were eager to talk about the test. One of the young girls asked another about a particular question.

The other girl said, "That wasn't on my test; maybe I completely missed it." It was at that moment we all realized there were several different test versions given to us.

I tried to make a joke by saying, "Well, congratulations, everyone. We have just succeeded in frying our last remaining brain cells by taking the hardest test ever designed." There was little reaction as everyone was exhausted, both physically and mentally.

We continued down the hall to a larger room. United States and California flags were at the front of the room on free-standing flagpoles, one on either side of a podium. In each of the four corners of the room, there were flags of the Navy, Army, Marines, and Air Force similarly displayed. We were instructed by an officer who had just entered the room to assemble in four uniform rows. We all then recited the Oath of the United States Military and were sworn in as members of the United States Armed Forces. There were congratulations all around the room.

After receiving our individual induction papers, now in nice new manila folders, we were escorted by guards down a hallway to a waiting bus that would transport us to overnight accommodations. Our last orders from the officer who swore us in were "to be on the last bus back to the MEPS facility at 7:00 a.m. or go to Leavenworth Military Prison for fifteen years."

We boarded the yellow school bus and made ourselves comfortable for the ride. I hoped the accommodations were close by. I was really tired; it had been a long day.

CHAPTER 6

GOOD NIGHT AND GOOD MORNING

I felt mentally exhausted and physically drained, more so than ever in my life. I could tell the other recruits felt the same; the bus was almost silent and void of any conversation. Comparing the SAT to the ASVAP tests is like comparing checkers to chess or even like comparing kindergarten to high school. I kept thinking about the four questions that I had left blank, and whether a better choice would have been to choose an answer. I was sure there was no absolute correct answer among the choices for those four particular questions.

It seemed to take quite a while to reach our overnight accommodations. It was close to midnight and it felt like the driver was driving us around on a tour of downtown Oakland. The thought crossed my mind that perhaps this was being done intentionally, so that we would not know the exact location of the MEPS facility or the overnight accommodations. Perhaps they needed more time to organize security at our destination.

I just wanted to take a shower and get a good night's sleep.

The bus pulled up and stopped at a six-foot-high wrought iron gate along the street. Two Military Police guards were present and opened the double gate inward. Within the gate was a nice swimming pool and concrete patio area. The lighting was not very bright, but I did notice guards, all with rifles, strategically placed around the perimeter.

Our busload of recruits filed though the gate and one young girl asked the closest MP, "Can we go swimming?" Her question broke the silence as many of us laughed. Several people began to talk about how hard the test was.

We were ordered to "file in" by one of the guards. About forty of us stood in a rough two rows facing a three-story wing of motel rooms. There looked to be about twelve rooms per level with armed guards at the ends on each floor. Behind the stairway, diagonally to our left, I saw a glass door. It was the side entrance to the part of the motel that was the office and dining area. To me, that part of the motel resembled a Denny's Restaurant in layout and appearance. I figured that was where we all would be having breakfast in six hours before going back to the MEPS facility. After completing the induction process, we would all be shipped out to our destination military bases for "A" school, depending on our job assignments.

A man in uniform approached us with a clipboard in his hand. He began calling out last names for room assignments. The young women were being paired and assigned to first floor rooms. The young men were being paired and most of them were assigned to the second floor. It seemed like some of the more "mild mannered" guys were put in first floor rooms that were not yet filled. Our group got smaller as recruits walked to their rooms.

I heard comments from some of the recruits entering their rooms like, "Hey, this is not bad," "This is kinda nice," and "Wow, I didn't expect this."

There were about eight of us left when I heard my name called with the room number 304. As I walked towards the stairway, I realized that no one was paired with me. Everyone else was on the first two floors. An MP with a rifle dropped in behind me as I started up the flights of stairs to the third floor of the building.

At the top of the stairs, I saw that room 304 was a couple doors to my right. Another MP with a rifle stood to the right of the door. The guard walking behind me took position left of the door as I entered the room and closed the door behind me. My room was the only one with guards stationed at the door, but I spent little time reflecting on this as I was way too tired.

In the room, there were two twin beds with nightstands and lamps. In the bed directly in front of me was a brown-haired young man, already asleep. I did not turn on the lights; there was enough ambient light coming through the curtains to navigate the room.

I wanted to take a shower before going to bed, but out of respect, I did not want to wake my roommate. I figured he must have been in an earlier group of recruits and he was just as exhausted as the rest of us. I would have plenty of time in the morning. The wake-up call would be coming in at 6:00 a.m. I would have an hour for a shower and breakfast before the last bus to the MEPS station departed at 7:00.

I removed my watch and wallet, placing them on the nightstand beside my bed along with the manila envelope containing my induction paperwork. I felt like something was missing and remembered that I had left my keys with my wife after dinner. I stripped down to my boxer shorts and crawled under the covers. Sleep was about the only thing on my mind at that point. I had to force myself to stop thinking about the test. It was done. I did my best. I felt I did fairly well. The bed was comfortable, and I fell into a deep sleep quickly.

Suddenly, I was awake. It must have been my internal clock telling me it was time to go. I grabbed my watch off the nightstand and saw that it was 6:58 a.m. I had synchronized my watch to the base's clock the night before, when we were sworn into service after the test.

In a loud voice I shouted, "Oh, shit! We didn't get a wake-up call! Wake up, dude! We only have two minutes to make the last bus!"

I completely startled my sleeping roommate. He jumped up quickly, reaching under his pillow, as if for a handgun. When he saw me franticly dressing and tying my shoelaces, he relaxed and laid back down.

"Come on, man! Move it! We're going to miss the last bus," I shouted.

He replied with, "YOU don't need this job."

As I grabbed my wallet and papers I said, "What the hell are you talking about? I am not going to prison for fifteen years because of your lazy ass! I have been out of work, and I have a two-year-old kid. Fuck this, I'm outta here!"

I sensed something was not right. Why was his initial reaction to reach under his pillow? Where the hell did he really come from? What did he mean by me not needing this job?

I burst out the door heading towards the stairs. As I looked down three stories at the configuration of the stairs I assessed my fastest exit. I saw six steps to the mid point 4' x 8' concrete landing on each level and six steps more returning back to the floor below me.

As I took my first step down, I decided to go two steps at a time. This screwed me up on the first set of six steps because I ended with one step to the landing. I had more than twice the momentum and speed than if I was running down them one step at a time. I nearly stumbled on the landing, almost twisting my ankle. I hit the railing with my left shoulder and rebounded to the second set of six steps down.

The second set of steps went better, three strides for six steps. I used a combination of 2-2-3 steps at a time. As I hit the second floor I bounced off the building wall, grabbed the railing and swung myself to the next set of steps. I took the next two sets of steps at three strides per set, bouncing off the landing's railing once again. I might as well have just jumped from the second floor because it took only six leaping strides to get to ground level.

Almost falling and off balance again, I ricocheted off the building at the ground floor. I headed for the glass door to the dining area that I had seen the night before, during room assignments.

I could hear several guards yelling "HALT" as I ran, but they couldn't catch me or even attempt to take aim at me with their rifles. I was moving faster than a ninja.

I yelled back, "How come I didn't get a wake-up call, you idiots?!" As I went through the single glass door, I could see through the dining room windows, the last bus idling at the curb with its doors open. I had less than thirty seconds to make that bus.

With my paperwork in my left hand, I zig-zagged through the tables and chairs in the dining area while I ran. I had the double glass front doors leading to the street in sight. There was almost no one in the room aside from workers clearing dishes and silverware from the tables.

A waitress lunged towards me and hooked my right arm with her right forearm to stop me as I passed. She called me by my first name and loudly said, "Please sit down and have a cup of coffee; everything is okay!"

As I spun myself clockwise to free myself of her grip, I loudly said, "How the hell do you know my name? What the hell is wrong with you people? Why didn't I get a wake up call?" I hated yelling at her because she was actually fairly attractive. I was facing her as I yelled, running backwards after breaking her grip. At this point, I was only a few feet from the front door.

I impacted the front door's push bar with my lower back, spinning clockwise again through the double glass doors. I ran for the open bus door less than thirty feet away. I could see recruits watching me through the windows of the bus and the driver could see me coming.

Suddenly the bus doors closed. The bus started to pull away and accelerate down the street as I was yelling for him to stop. Running alongside the bus, I could hear several people on the bus yelling at the driver to stop and let me aboard. I then saw two young girls, the ones that I had talked to before we took the test, rushing down the aisle towards the bus driver.

The girls started shaking the bus driver by the shoulders. They were yelling for him to stop and let me on as I was still running. The bus stopped abruptly.

As the bus doors opened, I yelled, "What the hell is wrong with you!?"

While I ascended the steps, the bus driver responded, "Please have a seat. I am sorry, sir. I am only following orders." I could see his right ear, but I could not tell if he had a communication device in his left ear. As I gasped to catch my breath, I thanked everybody for stopping the driver and swung myself down into an open seat.

One of the young girls asked me, "Why weren't you at breakfast, and why did you almost miss the bus?"

I told them all of what had just happened as everyone within range of my voice leaned towards me to hear the story. One young man asked me why I was sent up to the third floor when everyone else was on the first and second floors, but I had no answer for him.

The bus arrived at the MEPS facility very quickly. We must have taken a direct route for it seemed to be only about one city block away from the motel. I began to wonder if and why someone up high did not want me to make it to my induction into the military.

CHAPTER 7

UNBELIEVABLE

O ur bus had arrived at the rear entrance of the Oakland Military Entrance Processing Station. There were armed guards posted in several strategic locations around the building. As I exited the bus, I thanked the bus driver for stopping and letting me aboard.

He replied, "You are welcome, sir. Have a good day."

I followed the busload of recruits, entered the building and walked down a short hallway which opened into a large lobby. Folding tables were arranged in a rectangular U shape around the room with grouped letters of the alphabet marking where enlistees were to begin the final induction process.

I heard my first name called from across the room. A young brunette girl was walking towards me. She was the one that knew a lot about the background of the ASVAP and was telling the recruits about it before we took the test. We smiled at each other as she approached.

"We were looking for you at breakfast; what happened?" she asked.

I didn't want get into a long story, so I just told her that I never received a wake up call and barely made the last bus.

She followed with, "Did you hear the rumor that someone in our test group got a perfect score on the ASVAP?"

I said, "That's impossible!"

She then went on, "I think it was you. You were done early on almost every section of the test, especially the last section at the end.

You sat there and didn't turn in your test until a while after that other guy turned in his."

To this I replied, "You are incredibly observant." I felt flattered that she had been watching me during the test.

We both laughed as a guard motioned me to get in line, as all the lines were almost empty. We said our good-byes and gave each other a big hug.

As we hugged, I said into her ear, "You take care, young lady. Go get 'em. I can see you making officer training very soon."

We smiled at each other, both realizing that it was unlikely we would ever see each other again. She turned and headed into the physical exam area down another hallway.

The line for my last name was empty. A doctor in a white lab coat stood behind the table sorting through a stack of induction papers. He did not look up at me as he took the manila envelope I held out towards him.

He removed my papers from the envelope and immediately looked up at me, saying, "Son of Superman, what are you doing here?"

Once again I thought, "What is going on here?" I said, "Excuse me, sir, what do you mean by 'What am I doing here?'"

He gave me a serious look and said, "That point is now moot."

I instantly replied, "Sir, with all due respect, I believe a clerical error has been made. My father's name is Clarence, not Clark."

He responded with, "Son of Superman is what everyone here has been calling you since around midnight. The President and Chain of Command of the Department of Defense have given you that nickname."

His right hand reached to shake mine as he continued, "Congratulations, sir, you are the first person to ever achieve a perfect score on the ASVAP."

I replied with, "But that is impossible, sir."

The doctor continued, "And why is that, Mr. K?"

"Well, sir, there are questions on the test that are designed to slow you down, mathematical computations that take more than an hour each to solve, and there are also questions that do not have the answers in the choices."

"Exactly, let me see here (as he flipped though the pages of my files). You were given Version 5 of the test. Versions 3 and 5 are the most difficult. I personally feel 5 is much harder than all the others. I have not slept tonight because of you, so please bear with me here. You have put this country at DEFCON 4.

"You see, Mr. K, when the Department of Defense's mainframe computer graded your test it read your blank answers as blank, but when the four blanks matched the four questions that did not have answers on that test version, it shut itself down and all of the NORAD Defense System went black.

"The computer system that defends this country shut itself down. We thought this country was under attack. The Director of the CIA has accused you of being a foreign military spy. The computer had put out an error message that was never programmed into the system and shut down completely. What do you think about that?"

"Sir, it sounds to me like a brilliant software engineer considered, 'What if someone did get a perfect score?' and put in a backdoor subroutine to alert everyone. I can imagine the trouble he is in if that is the case."

"My thoughts exactly, Mr. K... You probably assume that I am just another doctor at this military installation. I am not. I am the Chief Physician of the entire Department of Defense. I am in charge of Army, Navy, Air Force, and Marines. Just by coincidence, I happened to be touring our nation's MEPS bases and was visiting here in Oakland this week. Do you know what MIT is?"

"Well, sir, it's not some Michigan Automotive Tech school. It is the Massachusetts Institute of Technology, renowned worldwide as the school that top geniuses attend. In fact, my father is a retired Department of Defense physicist, and the Navy put him through MIT for his degree in astrophysics after he was hired."

"Mr. K, I have three Ph.Ds from MIT—in mathematics, astrophysics, and medicine; and you make me and Einstein look like down-syndrome children!"

I hesitated a moment then said, "Sir, I am sorry, but I take some offense to your statement. I don't feel that it is acceptable to make light of those who have a disability over which they have no control."

"Well, okay, I will apologize for that, but you do understand the analogy I am making, don't you?"

"Yes, sir, and I am sorry for even making that comment," I replied, realizing the ramifications of the statement that this doctor had just made.

At that point, I realized that before me stood one of the most intelligent and influential men that has ever lived. I wouldn't be surprised at all if he was known as the smartest doctor on the planet, or even in some circles as the smartest man who has ever lived. I was overwhelmed with his analogy and told him so.

He continued, "There is no way I could have done what you did, even if the test had twice the time limit. How did you do that?"

"Well, sir, I cheated."

A shocked look appeared on his face because he knew that I knew I was going to prison if I had indeed cheated.

He said sternly, "How did you cheat?"

I replied, "Sir, I did not really cheat. What I mean by that is that most enlistees are eighteen to twenty-one years old, but I am thirty-one with about three years of college studies in the field of computer science. I have about a dozen years of life experience over all the others."

As he flipped through my files, he said, "You dropped out of Cal Poly in the early '80s and you have been working as a carpenter? You should have forgotten seventy-five percent of everything you learned by now because you do not work in technical fields and the like. Tell me this, what the hell are you doing pretending to be a carpenter?"

"Well, sir, I am a pretty good builder. I do all trades of construction and many refer to me as a master builder, auto and marine mechanic. My work was showcased in the *Better Homes and Gardens Architect Edition* a couple of years ago when I was a project manager building homes for celebrities in the greater Los Angeles area. I like to work with my hands, and I started a surfboard factory when I dropped out of college. I was ninety percent of the manufacturing process, as building surfboards is extremely labor intensive."

"What I meant was, why aren't you a top brain surgeon? And how dare you deny the human race your abilities! Why didn't you become a doctor or surgeon like me?"

"Well, sir, I gave that subject a lot of thought when I was younger. What it boils down to is that I never thought I could be comfortable with having someone's life literally in my hands. However, at this point in my life and after meeting you, I would pursue a medical career if I were given the opportunity and education."

The Chief Physician then said, "I can appreciate your sharing that with me as I spent weeks thinking about the same thing before I continued with my career."

As the doctor finished his sentence, I realized that the room was empty of recruits. There were only a handful of military guards positioned around the lobby.

The doctor then changed the subject with, "My superiors have ordered me to interrogate you. After meeting you, and considering our conversation so far, I do not feel that a formal interrogation is warranted. We are going to call this an informal interrogation. We are going to do this right now and right here. What I need from you now is honest and complete answers to every question I ask. Any deviation, and you will go to military prison. First question: Who at the Chrysler Corporation gave you the top secret mechanical drawings of the M1 Abrams Tank to study?"

"Huh? No one did, sir. My brother worked for Chrysler, but he only audited car dealerships. So that's what that transmission fit into! I knew it had to be big with all those hydraulics and reduction gear clusters."

"We checked out your brother thoroughly, and he had no access to such secret documents. He has been cleared. So, you are telling me that you did not study or ever see any mechanical drawings for the M1 Tank?"

I quickly replied, "Sir, mechanical things have always come naturally to me. I can pretty much fix just about anything except a human being."

"I figured that. You know, Mr. K, I spent several hours last night sitting in a room with over a dozen security experts and people like me, reviewing your test surveillance. Several individuals commented that it looked like you were the one who designed the whole damn tank! I don't think the people that did design it could go through those diagrams and questions that fast! You finished the mechanical section in less than fifty percent of the allotted time. Most people do not finish that section."

He continued, "I have another point to bring up. It was obvious to all of us present that you knew the test room was under surveillance. There were several people who wanted to discredit your perfect score, claiming that you did not follow orders. Case in point: No one has ever come close to completing the coding section. You are the only one to ever complete that section within the time allotted. In fact, one computer technician made the comment, 'I don't think our fastest super-computer could keep up with this guy!' You were filling in the last bubble and had it eighty percent colored in when the buzzer rang. Just for future reference, Mr. K, the computer would have read your choice with that much of the bubble filled.

"Now, I want you to know that a handful of us argued on your behalf. My argument was that you were in the process of filling in the last bubble of the coding section. So you did know the answer. You followed orders exactly by dropping your pencil at the buzzer. The people who wanted to discredit you also argued that you later went back and finished coloring in the bubble.

"Let me tell you exactly what you did, as shown by the security video. When your test was completed you closed the booklet and set it aside. You took the answer card and went over every bubble that you felt needed a complete mark to be read by the computer. You also noted on the scratch paper the numbers of the four questions that you left blank. Next, you set the answer card and pencil aside and never touched them again until you turned in your test. You were told at the start that you could not go back in the test booklet to work on previous sections. You looked for approval from the test administrator, then went back to those four questions in the test booklet and thought about each one for a long time. You did not work on your test.

"Some observers commented that you were 'putting on a show for us.' Since I am in charge of everyone on this base, nobody on this base outranks me, and what I say is the final decision, you did achieve a perfect score; and that is both final and official. Everyone is extremely impressed, to say the least. Now back to this interrogation. Have you ever traveled to or do you hold citizenship in or allegiance to any foreign country? Are you a foreign spy?"

"No, sir, I am not a foreign spy. When I was very young, our family traveled through Canada, but I really don't remember it. I have traveled to Baja California in Mexico less than ten times on surfing trips. Other than those instances, the only time I have left the continental U.S. is on family vacations to Hawaii."

He then said, "All that is fine and matches up to our records exactly. Very good. Next question: Are you an alien hybrid, have you been genetically altered, or are you a time traveler?"

"Sir?" I replied. This was really crazy that he would ask me this. **"We have found a deviation or abnormality in your DNA."**

At this point, my heart sunk deep in my chest. Thoughts ran through my head. "Was I abducted? Has he just confirmed to me the existence of extraterrestrial life? I might not be human! This can't be ..." I started to feel scared of what I might be.

I was a bit shaky when I asked, "Sir, am I a human being?"

He said, "Relax, you are a human, but definitely not the same as the rest of us. We have found something different with your DNA that no one can explain. I have also spent considerable time since midnight on the phone with the world's five top expert geneticists. None of them can explain or even theorize the modification or evolution of your DNA. They have already tried to replicate it, and they have also attempted cloning it. (At this point I was completely stunned. They had got a hair or something and extensively tested my DNA, tried to clone it already and had also tried to replicate it?) There is no possible way to reproduce your DNA deviation. Many in the scientific community believe that you have modified your own DNA and want to know how you have done it."

I said, "Sir, I am not an alien hybrid. This is crazy to me. A time traveler?"

"You do not exhibit the tachyon radiation that we theorize would be present with a time traveler; however, you will find this next part extremely interesting: About an hour ago I got two phone calls within minutes of each other. Earlier, last night, when none of the world's five top geneticists could explain or even theorize your DNA deviation, they all plugged your sample into their computer model programs to search for a possible match and explanation. These computers and programs have been running all night attempting to match your DNA. These are all diverse and separate individual computer model programs established by each geneticist. Two geneticists, one in Geneva and one in Germany, called to tell me that they have matched your DNA exactly with their computer model predictions of human evolution. Mr. K, they both matched your DNA at the same period of time, one thousand years in the future, exactly. We need to know what you have done to evolve a thousand years ahead of us."

"Sir, this blows me away! I am not a time traveler nor have I modified my DNA. I am a 'mutt,' referring to my racial mix of Hawaiian-Filipino and Caucasian. My father has the same IQ as Albert Einstein, and my mother is a schoolteacher who is extremely intelligent. All my siblings and I qualified for MENSA in elementary school when we were tested. Couldn't any of this offer some possible explanation?"

"No, all our extensive testing shows that your DNA has been modified since birth. Your DNA is not what it was when you were born. You have evolved one thousand years in thirty-one years of life. Let's save this topic for later. We have a lot to talk about. Come with me. You are not going through induction with the rest of the recruits. You are not in trouble. I am astounded by your knowledge and cooperation. Thank you. Walk down there and follow me please."

CHAPTER 8

FLYING COLORS

I walked left to the end of the row of tables and followed the Chief Physician towards a long hallway. On the wall, to the left of the hallway, I saw two older style wall-mounted telephones, circa late 1960s to early 1970s. One phone was the basic ivory-tan color with push buttons and the other was a dark red with no buttons or dial. The "Bat Phone" in the 1960's "Batman" television series crossed my mind.

As this thought was going through my head, the doctor said, "Please bear with me a moment. Wait right here; there is something I need to deal with immediately."

He picked up the handset of the red phone and within seconds he said, "It's me, sir." He paused briefly while the person on the other end of the line spoke.

The doctor looked at me and said, "He is right here in front of me, sir. I can say with utmost certainty that we can stand down from DEFCON 4. I will ask him now, sir; just a moment."

The Chief Physician laid the receiver to his chest and asked me, "Were there armed guards outside of your room? Did they order you to stop?"

I replied, "Sir, there were guards stationed, but none directly outside my door as I exited the room. Maybe they were taking a break, as all the other enlistees had already left for breakfast and the last bus. I heard them yelling for me to halt as I flew down the stairwell, but my final orders issued last night were to be on the last bus or go to Leavenworth Prison for fifteen years. I did not receive a wake-up call at 6:00 a.m. as promised, and I was desperate to make that last bus. The young man that was already in the room told me that I didn't need this job. Who was he?"

"Mr. K, he was a CIA agent planted in your room for security purposes."

The doctor had been addressing me very formally since our initial meeting, almost every sentence opened with "Mr. K" or "Sir." I asked him if it would be alright if he simply addressed me by my first name. He nodded his head and began to try to use my first name from that point on. Military formalities had to be maintained for the most part, but then again, standard protocol was broken anyway by my induction process being done individually.

He then put the receiver to his mouth and said, "He was simply following his last orders, sir... Yes, I agree, sir... incredible, sir... Yes, sir, all the MPs and agents are being questioned as we speak... No, sir, they cannot have him now. He has made it to this induction center, and he is now the property of the Department of Defense. Please tell them all to read up on our Constitution's by-laws. I will involve the Supreme Court in this matter if necessary, sir."

A couple of minutes passed while the other party spoke. From the doctor's facial expressions as he listened, it was obvious to me that there were discussions taking place on the other end of the call.

The doctor spoke again, "I am sorry, sir. Yes, they must do their job. My recommendations would be the same if I were there with you and not here, sir. No, I am confident that he presents no threat to your safety. Sir, I am convinced that he is the real thing... My apologies, sir, I was looking forward to it as well ... Yes, sir, I will be in touch later today with more information."

As the Chief Physician hung up the phone, he gave me a stern look as he said, "He is PISSED!" He took a deep breath and asked me, "Do you know who that was?"

I responded with, "I could make an educated guess, sir, but no, I do not know who that was."

The doctor asked me if I knew what 'Four Corners' was and I replied, "Four Corners is the only place in the United States where four states' borders intersect at ninety degrees."

He immediately requested, "Name them for me."

I quickly rattled off, "Utah, Colorado, New Mexico, and Arizona. Our family traveled across country every three to four years on vacations when I was young. By the time I was fourteen I had been to forty of the fifty states."

The doctor replied in a very serious tone, "I figured you knew that. That was the Commander in Chief on the phone. As we speak, Air Force One is making a U-turn over Four Corners. They are heading back to Washington D.C. because you somehow got past several armed guards and other agents, and made it to this induction facility. There is no way that the Secret Service will now allow the President in your presence. If you are, by remote chance, a foreign agent or assassin, there is no way anyone could protect the President, even with weapons trained on you. I am also very pissed off because you and I were supposed to be having breakfast aboard Air Force One as soon as they landed."

I replied with, "Sir, in hindsight, someone should have informed me of all of this."

He nodded his head in agreement with me. The Chief Physician's tone turned more friendly as he continued.

"So let's recap your accomplishments in the last few hours:

- First human being officially documented with an unmeasurable IQ and DNA advanced one thousand years ahead of the human race.
- First man ever accused of successfully infiltrating the United States Military by the Director of the CIA.
- Only enlisted man in UNITED STATES history, or any man for that matter, that any president has made an unscheduled flight to meet in the middle of the night during a war. This is also the first time a president has left his post as Commander in Chief during a war to meet anyone.
- And now, you are the only man in history that a United States president has ever been denied an audience with.

Quite a resume, I should say!"

He paused for a second as we stood there in the hallway. The doctor then proceeded to tell me in detail all the events that had transpired over the last seven and a half hours.

He started with the Department of Defense Mainframe Computer System shutting itself down at midnight when it graded my test. He elaborated on the conversations he had had with the software engineers and security experts concerning the error message that was not programmed into the system.

Next, he talked about the NORAD defense system going black, the country scrambling to DEFCON 4, and the conversations in the White House. He told me how he had been on the phone with the President numerous times since midnight. He then elaborated in detail on his conversations with the world's top five geneticists.

The Chief Physician told me that the directors of the CIA, NSA, and FBI were onboard Air Force One and had been debating with the President for the entire flight across the country. The primary topic of discussion was which agency was going to get me as an agent or operative.

As he concluded the chronological story of events, he said, "Off the record, I am glad that you made it here to this MEPS facility. One of my greatest fears was that one of those agencies would get you and turn you into a weapon. Worse than that, use you against each other. Since we are not having breakfast with the President now, maybe I can turn this into something beneficial for my colleagues and myself. If you would be interested, we can have lunch in my office later this morning and discuss how you have modified your DNA to be so far advanced ahead of the rest of us. We will talk about this later. Right now let's get you through the rest of your induction. There are some people I would like you to meet."

As we started to walk down the hallway, I saw four men wearing white lab coats standing by an open door. Stethoscopes around their necks and clipboards in hand, it was obvious that they were also important physicians of the MEPS facility.

I was introduced to the four other doctors. Each man was the head of each branch of the military at this Military Entrance Processing Station. Army, Air Force, Navy, Marines, and one of them was also the Head Physician in charge of the entire MEPS facility. I was in the presence of five of the most important doctors in the country.

Once again, the introductions were very formal and respectful. It felt kind of out of place to me. I was low man on the totem pole, a new recruit/enlistee, and all these men were high ranking officers who held extremely important positions in the military. I felt as if I were a dignitary or the President himself as I was greeted with, "Good morning, sir" and "It is such an honor to meet you." One of them even said, "I am so privileged to meet the Son of Superman."

The doctor closest to the doorway motioned with his hand for me to enter the room. It was like a classroom with desks moved towards the back corner to provide more space. Green chalk boards covered two walls. There was an oak podium in the front, which an attendant was positioning to face towards the center of the room.

One of the other doctors placed a stool in front of the podium and asked me to have a seat and get comfortable. The attendant took a seat on another stool and placed a book on the angled podium's top, which was facing me.

The book was fairly thick, maybe an inch and a half or so. It was bound at the top by two metal rings. Looking along the edge, the pages appeared to be thicker than average and plastic coated. The writing and logo on the cover were too small to read from my position on the stool.

The Chief Physician said, "Let's get started" and the attendant flipped the book's cover upward.

I immediately recognized the large colorfully dotted circle as the Color Blindness Test. I was relieved as I knew that I was not color-blind, and this was going to be easy. I was calling out one-digit numbers as fast as the attendant was flipping the pages.

After a short time, the numbers became two-digit and the Chief Physician ordered the attendant to turn the pages faster. I rattled off two- and three-digit numbers, catching my breath every four to six pages, or as the attendant slowed momentarily.

The Chief Physician had barked out, "Faster!" a couple more times in the first few minutes, and the attendant was struggling occasionally to turn pages as fast as he could.

This test was taking longer than any other color-blindness test I had ever taken in my life. I thought it was more than obvious that I was not color-blind. We were close to the end of the book. I was almost done. The attendant flipped the next page and I hesitated for a split second.

Instantly, the Chief Physician stepped towards me and said in a loud voice, "Why do you hesitate, Mr. K?"

I immediately answered, "Well, sir, in the warm colors, the red, orange, and yellow, I see the number fifty-six. At the same time, in the cool colors, the blue, green, and gray, I see the number seventy-two."

The room was silent as the attendant lifted the book and moved it back and forth in front of his face. He tilted it side to side before flipping the page over to see the correct answers, which were printed in fine type on the back lower corner of the card.

In a whisper, I heard him say, "No way" to himself.

The attendant then passed the whole booklet to the first doctor clockwise from his seat. Each doctor in turn viewed the picture carefully. They varied the distance and tilted the booklet in attempts to see both two-digit numbers. They then flipped the page over to view the answers on the back. Each had a look of amazement on his face as he passed it on to the next man. The fourth doctor passed the book in front of me to the Chief Physician, to my immediate left.

That doctor took only about two seconds to tilt the booklet and look on the back. All of a sudden the whole test booklet was airborne, like a Frisbee thrown hard sidearm. Fifteen feet away, the rocketing booklet hit the furthest back corner of the room, about six feet up the wall, with a loud BAM! as it exploded. The thick, colorful pages rained down like fallout, as if decks of cards were being used as confetti, some almost hitting the four doctors to my right.

Without hesitation, one of the doctors stepped forward, right in front of the Chief Physician's face, and said in a commanding tone, "I demand you apologize to Mr. K for your unbecoming behavior, sir!"

The expression on the Chief's face was one of "How dare you show insubordination to me in front of others," but it quickly changed as he realized what he had done.

My thoughts were that I needed to diffuse the tension in the room.

The Chief Physician instantly turned to me and said, "Mr. K, I sincerely apologize for my behavior which was uncalled for ..."

I interrupted him and said, "Doctor, there is no need for an apology as I take no offense to your actions. It is obvious to me that we are all in new territory here. Can we please drop some of the formalities and treat each other as equals?"

In retrospect, I have thought about the impact my actions and statements may have made on these men. Their hierarchy was based on rank and formal education parameters. Yet, a younger man who never finished college, with dozens of times their abilities, was reiterating the fact that we all need to treat each other as equals.

I still wasn't completely sure why the doctor had thrown the test book across the room. One of the other doctors must have noticed the puzzled look on my face and began to speak, "Before today, it was a universally accepted scientific fact that the human brain cannot process both ends of the visible light spectrum simultaneously. Right now, right here, you have just proved that 'fact' wrong. No one else that has ever taken a color-blindness test has seen both sets of numbers. Everyone sees one number or the other, never both, never simultaneously. Today you are changing accepted scientific facts. Your performance is amazing to all of us here this morning."

The tension in the room was now lifted. I felt comfortable in the company of all these doctors, and I sensed that they were comfortable with me.

The attendant who was turning the test booklet's pages asked the doctors, "What should I enter as a score?"

All the doctors looked at each other and the Chief Physician said, "200 plus."

The attendant began, "But, sir, the scale ends at ..."

The Chief Physician interrupted him. "I said 200 plus, just like everything else he has done today..." He then turned to me and said, "Well, let's get on with your induction."

As everyone began to move towards the door, I shook the hand of the attendant and thanked him. He smiled as we shook hands, then walked to the back of the room and began picking up the pages of the exploded test booklet.

The five doctors and I exited the room and started down the hallway to continue with the physical part of my induction process. The Chief Physician spoke as we walked, "Is there anything you would like to ask us, Mr. K? You have been bombarded with questions all morning, and you should have the opportunity to ask us questions. After all, we are supposed to be the doctors here."

I said, "Doctor, I realize as you have said earlier, that there is no way to measure my IQ. If you were asked to put a number value on me, by your superiors, what might it be?"

He stopped walking, as did the other four men. They all looked at each other and a couple of them shrugged their shoulders.

After a long pause, the Chief Physician said, "There is no way to determine your IQ. You aced the only test that could have given us any data to base our ability to come up with a number value. Let me think about this a bit more ... " He turned to the other four doctors and said, "Do any of you have any input to share on this subject?"

All the other doctors shook their heads from side to side in response.

The Chief Physician then continued after another long pause, "You do realize that the IQ scale ends at 200, and an IQ of 100 is the average human being. Using that scale I would make an educated guess that you must be somewhere between 5,000 and 10,000 on the scale of 200. Heck, I could be way off. You could easily be 30,000 for all I know. Hell, why are you asking me, I don't know shit compared to you."

He then asked the other doctors for their input. Two of them commented that the 5,000 to 10,000 range was a good estimate. They all reiterated that there was no possible way to come up with a "real"

IQ number for me. They all agreed that "unmeasurable" was the most accurate description of my abilities.

One of the other doctors then asked me, "Would you mind if we asked you a couple questions on a more personal level?"

I replied, "Sure, go right ahead, gentlemen." I wasn't really prepared for the questions they were about to ask, but I responded quickly to each question.

The first doctor opened with, "I really don't know how to best ask this, so I am just going to say it." He briefly paused before he continued, "What is it like to survive day to day among the rest of us? I mean, it must be worse than the movie 'Planet of the Apes' with Charlton Heston, or more like being stuck living on a planet of jellyfish?"

My instant reply was "Gee, thanks for putting that thought in my head; but seriously, I have never viewed myself in the position that you all put me in today. I have never thought myself to be more exceptional than anyone else. My personal feelings are that anyone who believes he is smarter or better than another has stupidity as his primary characteristic. Once an individual allows ego to supersede reality, all growth and balance is lost. That person has closed the door on open-mindedness and defeated his true potential."

They all reflected upon my answer for a moment. The Chief Physician then commented that I fell into the top 2% of all humans who have ever lived.

One of the others said, "More like 0.0002%, don't you think, sir?"

Several brief comments were offered by each person, then the Chief said, "One in ten billion of all humans that have ever lived is my estimate."

The other doctors all nodded in agreement.

At that point I interjected, "Gentlemen, while I too am having problems believing this is all real and not some dream, I must bring up this point. It is highly likely that other people exist with equal or even more 'gifts' than me. The ASVAP is only administered to recruits of the armed forces; it is not used in the general population."

After some silence, the conversation then continued to a discussion of the percentage of brain that is used by the average and above-average human being. Their discussion went on for a few minutes, and I listened attentively.

The final words from the doctors on this subject were, "Considering that ten to twelve percent of the brain is used by the average person and someone like Albert Einstein used twenty to twenty-five percent, you are definitely in the thirty to forty percent range. You could be as high as sixty to seventy-five percent usage or access. Once again, there is no definitive way to measure this. Today, you have forced us to change the way we look at everything. For example, after your performance today, an IQ of 200 really means nothing anymore."

One of the doctors looked at me and started to ask a question. "I am very uncomfortable in asking you this next question, but many of my colleagues have religious beliefs and we feel the need to ask you this. Please forgive me for asking, but are you the second coming of Christ?"

Through my mind flashed, "How do I even begin to respond to this man?"

But I instantly replied, "Sir, being that I was raised as a child in the Roman Catholic faith and had to attend catechism until I was about eighteen years old, I would have to consider such a thought crossing my mind to be a sign of undeniable delusion and mental illness. I myself believe in a more universal view of all religions, that in fact none of them is completely correct. All hold common teachings and views. All religions hold only pieces to the complete puzzle or real truth; combined they hold the true picture. Let's assume for a moment that the Christian faith is 100% fact and truth. If Christ were to come again, do you really think he would tell anyone he was here? I mean, look what happened to him the first time."

My response seemed to quell a discussion that I did not want to enter into at that point in time. Once again, all the doctors paused for a while to contemplate my response to the question.

A different doctor made another point, "You do realize that you fit the classic textbook definition of 'crazy,' don't you? What I mean is that a human being with an unmeasurable IQ and DNA that is advanced 1,000 years ahead of the rest of us is just impossible, yet here you stand in front of us, clear as day. I really appreciate spending this time with you, sir."

I replied, "The honor has been mine, gentlemen. I could never have dreamed of meeting such extraordinary men as yourselves. I really wish we could simply carry on our conversations like this for hours, or days."

We all shook hands again as the four doctors excused themselves to return to their daily routines at the MEPS facility. I would continue the rest of my physical exams with the Chief Physician alone.

Down the hallway, we entered a room and I sat facing an eye chart. The Chief Physician asked me to cover one eye at a time and asked me to read the lines near the very bottom of the chart.

When we were done, he said, "Forty over twenty. Do you know what that means? The first number is the distance you can recognize the letters. The second is the average person's ability. In other words, you have twice the vision as other people who have what we consider to be perfect eyesight."

He then picked up an otoscope (a device used to examine the ear) off the counter.

As he started to look into my left ear, I said, "Doctor, please excuse my ears as I did not get the opportunity to take a shower this morning, without that wake-up call."

He replied, "Don't worry about it. Do you swim a lot? I see some closure in your ear canal."

"You mean exostosis?" I said.

"You know what exostosis is? Tell me what exostosis is, Mr. K."

I replied, "Exostosis is the growth of calcium deposits along the ear canal, generally caused by the rapid cooling of the inner ear by water evaporation. A common name is 'Swimmer's Ear.' I did tell you earlier that I used to surf almost every day, Doctor."

"Excellent answer. Where did you learn all these things you know? You have no history of any pre-med or medical school?" His question seemed to be rhetorical by his tone, so I did not answer him.

After a few more physical tests like the duck walk, reflex response, and the classic "turn your head and cough," my blood was drawn.

"That wraps it up," he said. "You are in exceptionally good shape for your age, or any age for that matter. So, what do think about lunch in my private office so that we can talk about genetics and evolution?"

"That sounds fine to me, Doctor," I replied as I followed him down another hallway to his personal office.

CHAPTER 9

LUNCH WITH THE DOCTOR

As we walked to the Chief Physician's office, he explained to me that he had his own private office in every major Military Entrance Processing Station in the United States. He once again shared the fact that there was no surveillance whatsoever in his office. He wanted me to be honest and forthcoming with all that I might contribute to his knowledge base.

We entered a nicely furnished office, and he asked me if I wanted something to drink. He mentioned that he even had imported beers in his small refrigerator. He said if I would like one, he would join me in a beer.

I replied, "Doctor, I must have had over five pitchers of Bud Lite with the recruiters at dinner last night, so a beer doesn't really sound good right now. I wouldn't mind a soda though." He then said, "Are you hungry? We could have a New York steak with all the trimmings if you like. The food here is excellent!"

"Well, I'm not really hungry right now, Doctor, but you go ahead and eat. After all, you have been up all night. Please don't worry about me," I said.

He replied with, "I think I will head home after our meeting, and I can wait to eat. Yes, I am very tired, but I am eager to hear the things you have to share with me."

We must have talked for over three hours. The doctor started out by telling me a couple of stories from his college days to assure me there were no surveillance devices present, though it's not my place to share those accounts. He wanted me to feel comfortable discussing anything and everything that came to my mind.

The first subject we discussed was all the chemicals and drugs I had been exposed to or experimented with in my life. I started by telling him how I helped my father paint the house when I was about twelve years old. Back then, people had mercury added to the oil-based paint to help prevent mildew. When painting the eaves of the house, the paint would run down our arms—and that required the use of paint thinner or turpentine to clean up.

I then brought up another story from my younger years. When I was about fourteen years old, we had an extreme black ant infestation. My father told me he had insecticide concentrates stored somewhere in the garage. I used a chemical called Chlordane and mixed the spray solution at double or triple strength. I believe that the use of Chlordane was banned a few years after DDT was. I must have sprayed over a dozen gallons of mixed insecticide on the property. I sprayed the foundation of the house and every landscape plant and lawn border. I covered every fence line and walkway edge, including the driveway and street.

We did not have ants for over twelve years. When the black ant population began to reappear, they were one-third their normal size and their exoskeletons were almost transparent. Years later, I was amazed the black ants were able to eventually overcome the dose of Chlordane that I had used.

Next, I talked about the petroleum products used in the automotive and marine industries. Especially important are the lighter solvents and chemicals, as they can be absorbed into the body through the skin. From there I went into the chemicals involved in surfboard construction. The catalyzing agent for setting off the chemical reaction required for the polyester resin of fiberglass to harden is called methyl-ethyl ketone peroxide.

MEK peroxide is an oxidizing agent and very dangerous. One drop of this catalyst splashed into the eye could result in permanent blindness within ten seconds.

Using latex gloves was a standard procedure when working with any dangerous chemicals, but sometimes I was careless. I would often get this oxidizing chemical on my hands. Washing with soap and water became very tedious and time consuming. I began using the solvent acetone to rinse these spills from my hands. The problem with acetone is that it readily permeates through the epidermis and can transport chemicals directly into the bloodstream.

I also brought up the chemicals in many different automotive paints and their respective solvents. From lacquers to acrylic enamels, two-part epoxy paint systems and the like.

Occasional exposure to all these chemicals is tolerable, especially when safety equipment like gloves and respirators are used and maintained. We briefly discussed the possible mutations that might occur due to extended use of and overexposure to all of these chemicals. He did not feel any of these were responsible for the deviation in DNA that was found. He did make the point that my repeated exposure to all these chemicals over the years might create potential health issues later on in life.

Next, I brought up some subjects that I wanted to discuss. The first topic was the Chernobyl nuclear incident and the contamination of the entire planet. I told him how I felt that the long-term effects of this one event could create problems for a significant percentage of the population, decades in the future. We talked for a while about this and radiation-related subjects. We talked about oversights in engineering designs and possible actions to minimize future accidents.

I brought up my perspective that cancer will never be cured. Although research leads to more effective treatments, cancer is more akin to evolution than a disease. Cancer is an undesirable mutation of living cells on a biomolecular level. Evolution is also mutation based, although evolution is a positive mutation lending towards the survival of any species. This conversation continued on both sides, and I brought up my thoughts that evolution is also driven by a conscious need rather than just by biochemical reaction to environmental changes or biological needs. Evolution can be driven forward quickly, and not always over periods of thousands of years. I theorized that my DNA deviation might be an evidence of this. I also shared my thoughts that, "Most people do not realize that the mind carries the body, not vice versa."

At this point, I break from my story to share my personal perspectives on recreational and pharmaceutical drugs. No drug will enhance intelligence or ability long-term. While some hallucinogens may temporarily enhance neural connections of the brain in a percentage of the population, these effects are short-lived and could have dangerous or undesirable side effects, even death. These "enhancing" drugs do affect the brain on a biochemical level, but it is far better to reach these "openings or enhanced connections" by meditation or experience. Training the brain to use "doors opened" is another completely separate topic for discussion. The use or experimentation of recreational drugs is a personal choice, and I do not condone or approve experimentation on oneself.

I assume no responsibility for any reader who takes my experiences and discussions with others out of context. Were I to be completely forthcoming regarding this topic, I feel a reader would need to have a deep background in biochemistry, medicine, genetics, psychology, neuroscience, etc., in order to be objective and responsible with all the information I could give. Since such knowledge is atypical for most readers, I have chosen not to share my thoughts on this subject in their entirety—though I will proceed a bit further.

A large percentage of the population fall prey to drug and alcohol addiction. You will find that most intelligent people have some method of self-medication.

"To come up with a solution, one must first define the problem."

Open up, talk to close friends. Define the problem. Most times, the true problem is NOT abuse or addiction. These are simply symptoms. Something else is wrong that you are not dealing with. If you solve that problem first, you will no longer feel the need to anesthetize yourself to these buried or ignored problems. Self-medication is a crutch, nothing more.

Many of these crutches are acceptable in modern society. Once again, one must break the conditioning and evolve beyond accepted norms.

"You can't face the music if you don't hear it playing."

There is no better feeling than overcoming something that has bound your progress and spirit just because you procrastinated or refused to face it. Human beings have been limited by the conditioning of society and civilization. Believe in yourself. Empower yourself. Reality is what you make it. Impossibility is an imprinted mindset. Go beyond perceived limitations. Step up and confront situations that you are afraid of. Build your self-confidence. Stand up for your beliefs.

Communicate honestly with those you share life with. Life is too short and too precious to cloud the positive energy that comes from deep, truthful communication. The positive energy you share is felt and amplified by those around you. Your energy forces the energies of others to surface, naturally. Be an example for others. Do not give up on yourself; be an inspiration to those around you.

For the reader to get a broader sense of my exchange with the Chief Physician, there was a television special aired on the History Channel perhaps a decade ago. This special contained many of the subjects the doctor and I discussed at length, over twenty-five years ago. The title of the special was "The God Gene."

I then shared my experimentation in my college years with the doctor. Both of us agreed from personal experience that none of the drugs and chemicals, whether organic or synthetic, provided any contribution or explanation for the deviations or abilities observed. We covered about everything anyone could think of.

This part of the discussion went on at length and at the end he said, "If there is one thing that sticks out in your mind, I would like to hear it."

I replied (in relation to one organic hallucinogen), "Most do not know that saliva is the chemical component which modifies this organic hallucinogen to be one carbon-oxyhydroxide molecule off of serotonin, which is naturally occurring in the human brain. Serotonin is believed to be responsible for many 'sixth sense' abilities. The saturation or substitution of such a similar chemical chain might lead to certain abilities being unlocked."

To this he replied, "How the hell did you know that? I am the one with the MIT Ph.D., yet you are telling me things that I don't know ... I am supposed to be the expert!"

I told him about a book I had read while attending college, and about the background of the author. The Chief Physician told me that he was very familiar with this other doctor's work in the field, but had never heard about this particular book. He immediately got on the phone to one of his aides. He asked them to acquire the book and have it on his desk by morning.

The doctor closed our meeting by discussing some peripheral information in regards to me. First was a brief discussion of reasons why the government felt that the world should not be told of my existence, setting aside the obvious reasons of National Security. One comment the doctor made was "Imagine what your life might be like if everyone was on your doorstep asking you to solve their problems, you would have no private life, to say the least." Another pertinent comment he made was "Most of us feel that the majority of the human race would never be able to accept the fact that you actually exist with your abilities."

He said, "You must realize that now, since your abilities are known to us (the government), many people will have their eyes on you. I am going to make it my personal responsibility to see that you are never used as a lab rat for experimentation. I will have people watching the people watching you in order to determine their intent and goals. You and your family will be watched over and protected. I personally give you my word and assurances."

He continued, "You have shown us so many new things, and many suspect that you have abilities which you are not sharing. I don't want to know if you do. No one else needs to know anything more than what you are willing to freely share. You have already given us information that will take years to explore and investigate. Now, I am extremely exhausted, please forgive me. Let me walk you down to induction and get you set up with the job of your choice. You qualify, or actually are over-qualified, for any job in the military. What are your preferred choices?"

I said, "With my background in math and computer science, Fire Control is my best choice according to the recruiters."

He replied, "That is an excellent choice for you. That job also requires the top psychologically balanced recruits as well, and you meet and exceed all conditions."

We left his office and walked through a series of halls into a large open room with office desks. Uniformed men sat at each desk with computer terminals, assigning jobs and verifying qualifications for all enlistees. They assigned destination military bases, "A" school enrollment and departure from the MEPS that same afternoon.

The Chief Physician and I shook hands and he told me, "If you get hungry or need anything, just tell anyone in this room. Someone will bring you whatever you want from the cafeteria downstairs."

He wished me well and made sure that several of the people in the room acknowledged his words to me. He made the statement that "our paths would cross again and we could relax and chat further in the future."

A spot opened at one of the desks and a man in uniform said, "Son of Superman, I can help you over here."

When he made that statement, several enlistees in the room looked over at me. Apparently, the rumor that somebody had received a perfect score on the ASVAP the previous night was main topic of interest throughout the whole facility that day. Those who stopped to look over at me or lingered were ushered from the room quickly by military guards.

CHAPTER 10

A HARD CHOICE

I sat down in a comfortable chair positioned alongside the enlisted man's desk. We began to talk about job assignments as he looked through my documents.

He said, "What am I doing? I don't need to review your files. I know who you are and what you have done here today. You can have any job you want. What will it be?"

I answered, "Fire Control."

He replied with, "Good choice! Oh, by the way, your recruiters in Santa Rosa have been calling all morning to congratulate you. Apparently, Command is thanking them for finding you. Let's get this done, and I will get them on the phone for you."

The enlisted man pecked away at his keyboard and finally asked, "What's going on here? This can't be right. This system is telling me that Fire Control is impacted, and there is no opening for 'A' school in Chicago right now. Let me get on the phone. Pick up that other phone, and you can talk to your recruiters while I figure out what's going on here."

I picked up the receiver of the desk phone nearest me and was connected to the recruiting office up in Santa Rosa. All three of my recruiters were on the line talking over one another as they offered their congratulations on my test score and achievements.

One said, "Dude, how was breakfast on Air Force One? Shit, we knew you were smart, but you blew everyone away. Holy shit, man!"

I told them that the President had to turn back to Washington before their arrival, and someone would probably tell them the story later. I told them I was choosing my job at the moment, but there seemed to be some sort of problem. At that moment, the clerk interrupted us and we had to get off the phone for a few minutes.

He informed me that he had just spoken to the base in Chicago and, though it had never happened before, there was no opening for five months. Then he offered me other job choices which included becoming a medic or a doctor or an aircraft mechanic, along with many other possibilities. Though my recruiters and other military personnel had convinced me that Fire Control was the best fit for me, I responded, "Sir, my second and third choices would be fighter pilot or Navy SEAL; but I have been told that these positions are not open to me because of my age."

He replied with, "First off, don't address me as sir. I am an enlisted man, just like you are now. In fact, in a few months I'll be addressing you as sir because you have a fast track to officer's training already in your file. Physically and in every other way, you are more than qualified for your other choices.

"The reason your age limits your ability to become a SEAL or pilot is because of the training involved and the expected service duration. A pilot or SEAL is expected to do over a decade of service once they are trained. This is the reason for the age threshold. The Navy knows you have the potential to be an outstanding pilot or SEAL, but for the amount of training invested, you would probably be less effective eight to ten years from now. How about the medical field? Become a doctor or surgeon."

"I am not prepared to make that decision now that Fire Control isn't an option right now," I said. "I expected to ship out today. What I am supposed to do for five months? I am no better off than I was a few days ago."

"The best I can do is schedule you to ship out to Chicago in May. Where do you want to depart from?"

I hesitated ... I had a big problem. "I went through all of this so I could have my job by the end of the day ... and now Fire Control doesn't have an opening until May? Where am I going to put my family? I can't impose on my in-laws for five more months. I expected my wife and son to be relocated with me in a couple months after my schooling. In one sense, I now have more problems than I did yesterday ... and how do I get back to Ukiah?"

His reply was, "If you want to ship today, you have to choose a different job. If you want to stay with Fire Control, which I think you should, I will get the guys in Santa Rosa to come get you and drive you back to Ukiah if necessary."

I was frustrated and a little angry, to say the least. After all the excitement and everything that had happened in the last sixteen hours, I now felt worse off than I did days ago. I asked to speak with my recruiters and the enlisted man handed me the telephone receiver as he dialed numbers.

I opened my phone conversation with "I have a problem, guys. Fire Control doesn't have a school opening for five months ... "

The conversation went on for several minutes, and my recruiters asked me to hand the phone over to the clerk. Voices got so loud on the phone that I could hear parts of their conversation from where I sat.

About twenty minutes later, the resolution was that my Santa Rosa recruiters were on their way to pick me up, and they would call my wife to see if she could drive down from Ukiah to pick me up from their office. I was not happy about any of this.

I told the clerk that it would probably be best to schedule my departure to "A" school in Chicago from Los Angeles International Airport in May. I told him that I would probably have to move my family down to southern California to stay with family there until they were relocated by the Navy to be with me. I told him that I would stay in contact with my recruiters and advise them of any changes.

The clerk punched everything into the computer and printed out my departure information. I ended up sitting at his desk and chatting with enlisted men in the room for almost two hours while we waited for the guys from Santa Rosa to arrive.

It was after sunset when the call came that two of my recruiters were waiting at the back of the MEPS. I was escorted out the back entrance of the building where the bus had dropped us off early that morning. When I stepped into the Chevy minivan, I greeted my recruiters and thanked them for driving down to pick me up and asked why they weren't in the Ford Aerostar.

The driver said, "This is what the motorpool had for us; we don't get to choose. Heck, with what you did today, the Navy should be driving you around in a limousine!"

We all laughed as we made our way out of Oakland and across the Bay Bridge to Highway 101 North. The men soon asked me to tell them the whole story about everything that had happened since they dropped me off, about twenty-four hours prior. They really wanted to know why Air Force One turned back, but after telling them about the events at the overnight accommodations, they soon had their answer.

One of the guys spun off on a tangent, talking about how much trouble all the MPs and agents were in for letting me escape the motel room and make that last bus. Once they realized I hadn't eaten all day, we went through a fast food drive-thru for burgers and fries somewhere near Petaluma, north of Oakland. The drive north went relatively fast, and when we pulled up at the front of the recruiting office in Santa Rosa, my wife was already there, waiting in the truck. She got out and gave me a hug, and I thanked her for driving down. We said goodnight to the guys and started on the two-hour drive back to Ukiah.

During the drive, I didn't tell her anything except that my job opening was not for five months. She told me her parents were set on believing that I was rejected by the Navy. She then began to tell me she and her mother were not getting along and she was desperate to get out of her parents' home. Before we arrived back in Ukiah well after midnight, we had formulated a game plan to return to southern California.

I recall sleeping in that next morning, exhausted from the previous day's events. My young son woke me up in the late morning with, "Daddy, breakfast is getting cold and Grandma and Grandpa are anxious to talk to you."

On the dining room table was a plate of bacon and eggs. My mother-in-law brought me a cup of hot coffee then sat down by her husband. My wife joined us after leaving my son playing with toys in the other room.

Then, her parents' barrage began. "So, the Navy rejected you. What are you going to do now? How are you going to support your family? You say that construction is slow around here, but how do we know that you have even actually been looking for work over the past weeks?"

I sat in silence as they got it all out of their system. I respected what they had to say, but with what had just transpired in the last thirty-two hours, they should have been in awe of me. It would have been funny if they had known what had transpired and that the President had flown half way across the country to meet their son-in-law. Some of the degrading comments and tones made me want to smack them both upside the head, but I maintained my composure and resolved to tell them very little of what had happened. They would never believe it anyway. Who would?

I calmly started in, "Let me know when you two have finished, so I can have the floor. I have a lot to say. Things happened that you would never believe, but basically none of you have the security clearances to hear any of it anyway. Once you two are done ripping me, I need about thirty minutes to talk."

They both looked at me as if disgusted with my arrogance as my father-in-law said, "Okay then, what do you have to say?" My wife sat there with a blank look on her face. I think she had been out in the garage smoking pot and playing with the dogs when our son woke me. I could smell the faint odor of marijuana as she sat next to me. I was a bit angry with her for smoking pot while we were at her family's home. She actually believed that her parents couldn't smell it and didn't know she was high. She was being very disrespectful to her parents, especially after all the conversations that had transpired over recent weeks.

I calmly began, "I can not begin to thank you enough for allowing us to come up here and stay with you. I want you to know that I passed on an offer of a fifty percent ownership in a major construction company and a six-digit annual salary to try to save this marriage and keep this family together for the sake of your grandchild. The main reason we came up here was to get your daughter away from the less-than-acceptable crowd that she has been associating with.

She and I have separated and reconciled five times in the last six to eight months. I am sorry I have been unable to find employment. In desperation I have joined the Navy for a job, and I have a very good one. I do not ship out for five months. I will take my family to southern California within the next two days to stay with my family. My job assignment is Fire Control, which means I would have the responsibility of pushing the firing button on a Nuclear Tomahawk Cruise Missile. In case you don't realize it, a person has to be among the smartest and most psychologically balanced people ever tested to be assigned to that job. That is who I am.

"I have listened to you call me an irresponsible loser and even a lowlife or worse to my face over the last few weeks. The President of the United States flew to meet me last night. If you knew everything that transpired while I was gone, you'd probably both have a heart attack—but I won't tell either of you or your daughter what happened because the occurrences of the last thirty-two hours are classified.

"I am now held in the highest regard by the Department of Defense and the United States Government. This family is now watched over and protected by many institutions of the United States because of me. You have no idea, nor will you probably ever know the full extent of that statement.

"I will not tolerate any further verbal or psychological abuse directed at your daughter or at me. Yes, obviously, she needs more time to live up to promises she has made to all of us (we all saw her swollen, red eyes), but I care about her and our family. We will leave your home within two days. Today, I will take everything in the storage unit to the dump. There is nothing there of any real value. I am almost completely out of money, but I will ask you for nothing. You have been more than supportive of us for these past few months. For this, I am personally indebted to you.

"I know you and your daughter have not been on the best terms for years, but I feel this alienation and lack of compassion has to stop. Although I am speaking in a calm tone, I am so damn pissed off about what has been going on here that it makes me sick to my stomach. Your daughter needs time, love, and understanding to make the changes she tells us she wants to make. Sure, I could have walked away from her when she first filed divorce papers. I could have had sole custody of our son because of some of the shit she has pulled over the last few months. (At this point, my wife burst into tears and ran from the room). I love her and care about her and know that somewhere inside she is the woman I married. Your grandson needs both parents, together. I forgive your daughter. I forgive you, for you do not know the truth about everything. You actually know very little and what you think you do know is so far from the truth that you couldn't accept it. I don't really care what you think of me at this point. My concern is my immediate family, and this is no place for them right now.

"Once again, I thank you from the deepest part of my heart for putting a roof over our heads for the last few months. I owe you. Right now, I am heading to the storage unit and taking our son with me. You and your daughter have things to work out alone. We will be back before sunset. I will even take Pepper with us. I know your daughter will want to keep Aussie here with her. I apologize for raising my voice; I love both of you. That is all I have to say right now. We have a lot to do in the next forty-eight hours."

My in-laws sat in stunned silence. Before long, my wife's mother went to the bedroom to check on her daughter. I saw my son standing in the doorway of the living room.

My almost three-year-old son had a worried look on his face as he asked, "Daddy, is everything okay? Is Mommy okay?"

In an extremely calm tone I responded, "Yes, Son, everything will be okay. I am sorry Daddy's voice got loud. Do you want to go with Daddy to the storage unit? On the way back we can stop and get a Happy Meal."

He was immediately excited and asked, "Daddy, can Aussie and Pepper come with us and ride in front? There is plenty of room if it's just you and me."

"Well, I think Aussie should stay with Mommy. Why don't you go to Mommy right now and get your shoes and jacket while Daddy puts your car seat back in the truck. You make sure you tell Mommy that you and Daddy love her and that we will be back soon."

My son and I drove to the outskirts of Ukiah, to the storage unit and dump. It took two truckloads to the dump to get rid of the washer, dryer, refrigerator, master bedroom furniture and assorted furnishings. I saved the pictures, valuables, and clothing for the last load because they were going with us. The truck was packed above the side rail metal toolboxes, almost up to the lumber rack bars. I tied off everything well and put a tarp over the load as it looked like rain or snow might be on the way, and the truck was ready for the 1,000-mile drive to southern California.

If we could have fit everything in the truck, I would have put my wife's Toyota Celica on consignment on a car lot in Ukiah; but we had too much stuff back at the house as well as the two Australian Shepherds. We would have to take both vehicles, packing everything else in her car; but I wasn't sure I had enough money left to put gas in both cars for the whole trip, especially after paying dump fees and the final storage unit bill.

We stopped at the local fast food restaurant for my son's Happy Meal. Though I didn't eat, my son did insist that I buy a regular hamburger for Pepper and another to bring home for Aussie.

Arriving at the house, I asked my son to go feed the hamburger to the other dog and ask Mommy to come outside to talk to me. I rearranged the load on the truck and tied a second rope over the top of the tarp.

My wife came out the front door with two suitcases, obviously on the same page as I was. She immediately saw that the truck was full and that we would be taking both vehicles, so she put the suitcases in the back seat of her Celica. I saw that she had already packed everything except the dogs' food and water bowls. She said she couldn't be around her mother for another minute and wanted to leave before sunset. Her dog, Aussie, was bouncing around excitedly. He had just finished off his hamburger and had figured out we were going on a road trip.

My wife's parents had never seen that side of me. I was an easy-going guy and had been passive and humble despite their words over the last few weeks. They had no idea of the kind of man I was, and I think they were afraid of me after I reacted to them at the breakfast table earlier. I approached my father-in-law up on the front porch.

Very peacefully, I said, "Sir, I sincerely apologize for my tone earlier. I am also sorry to have brought my family's problems to your home. Please forgive us. We do love you guys. It is obvious that the women are not getting along, so we will be on the road shortly."

He said "You don't have to leave tonight. Come in and have dinner. Get a good night's sleep."

"I think it's best we get on the road. I have enough to get a motel room later tonight. The dogs can sleep in the truck. Once again, I thank you for having us and trying to help us. This is my responsibility, and I will compensate you as soon as I am able. I hope that after a short time, this can all be forgotten and considered water under the bridge. All the straws have just built up on the camel's back for far too long. I am sorry things didn't go as planned, but I do have everything laid out in front of me. We can talk later when things cool off. Please tell your wife we love her. I'm going to send your grandson in to spend time with you until we're ready to pull out. I'm sorry; I do respect the both of you."

He reached out his hand to shake mine and said, "You have been so quiet over the last few weeks, your words this morning caught us by complete surprise. I see that you are not angry, and you must do what you must. I know you are a good man, and I realize the position you are in. I respect you, too, and I am sorry we couldn't help more. You guys drive safely, and please call when you arrive at your folks' house so we know you're safe."

My wife took our son into the house to spend a few minutes with his maternal grandparents while she retrieved the last of our things. My wife got in her car with her dog, Aussie, and I loaded our son into his car seat next to me with Pepper riding shotgun. The sun was just touching the mountaintops at the horizon as we departed the circular driveway. I could see tears pouring from my in-laws' eyes up on the porch as my son waved and yelled good-bye to his grandparents from his car seat next to me.

CHAPTER 11

THOUSAND MILE DRIVE

We pulled into a gas station to top off both cars' gas tanks before heading south on Highway 101. My wife's car was half full, as it had rarely been driven since we arrived in Ukiah. The truck was bone dry, requiring almost twenty-two gallons to fill it. I went to the payphone to call my recruiters after the cars were filled. My wife parked on the side of the gas station, and I saw her lighting up a joint while I was on the phone. This was no time to confront her about it. Our son was riding with me, and she was under a lot of stress; I decided to let it go. At that moment she looked up and realized that I had seen her.

One of the recruiters was still in the office and answered the phone. I told him about our situation and that I was short on cash. He told me to meet him at the office when we passed through Santa Rosa in two hours or so.

I then called my parents and explained the situation. My father told me to call him when we stopped somewhere with access to a Western Union Office so he could wire me enough money to make it home.

After getting off the phone, I walked over to my wife's car. As she rolled down the window, I could see and smell the pot smoke, but I didn't mention it. We decided that she would lead and I would follow her until we got close to Santa Rosa. From there I would lead to the recruiting office downtown. I told her that one of the recruiters would meet us there to either loan me some money or help us find an open Western Union Office. We decided to stay within five to ten miles of the posted speed limit, because we basically had a two-day drive ahead of us. We agreed on signals using brake taps or flashing high beams when we needed to stop to let the dogs out or take a break.

We arrived in Santa Rosa around 9:00 p.m. The military recruiting office was closed and the door was locked, but a car pulled up behind us a few minutes later. It was Joel, one of my recruiters. He unlocked the office as I summarized what had transpired earlier that day. We tried to locate an open Western Union office by telephone, but had no luck. We ended up driving to the nearest gas station where Joel topped off both of our tanks using his credit card and loaned me the sixty-five dollars he had in his pocket. I owe all my recruiters a huge debt of gratitude for everything they did for me—especially what was to happen five months later. They were a great group of guys.

Back on the highway, we traveled to just north of the San Francisco Bay area and then headed east to reach Interstate 5 South. It was well after 1:00 in the morning; the truck needed gas and we needed a break after over seven hours on the road, so we pulled into a rest area. I had only about eighty dollars left, and everyone was hungry and tired. We fed the dogs their remaining dog food, and our son ate some cheese and crackers that my wife had brought along. But we needed a good night's sleep, so we headed for a small roadside town just south of us where I knew there were several motels and dining establishments.

The Central Valley fog was getting heavy. Visibility on the road was less than forty feet, and the traffic was extremely slow. A few miles down the road, we pulled into a reasonably priced motel; I had just enough money to get us a room for the night and buy a few burgers to feed the family. The motel had a Western Union counter, so I called my parents collect from a payphone. Money would be available in the morning.

After filling our gas tanks and eating a big breakfast at a nearby Denny's the next morning, we were on the road again by 10:00 a.m. We stopped at rest areas along Interstate 5 every two or three hours and spent more than a half hour each time letting the dogs run and stretching our legs. The last couple of weeks had been incredibly stressful on all of us.

We arrived at my parents' home in Ventura County just before midnight, and they welcomed us in. My mother already had one of the larger bedrooms all set up for us. The dogs were happy because they were allowed in the house, and my parents actually owned one of Pepper's puppies, which was now about eight years old. Of my five younger siblings, only my youngest sister still lived at home in the six-bedroom house.

Without the stress that was present in my wife's parents' home, we all got a good night's sleep. I was just relieved to have my family in my childhood home.

CHAPTER 12

FIVE-MONTH STRETCH

I woke early the next morning and got out of bed without waking my wife and son. The dogs followed me, and I let them out into the large unfenced yard. They were good about staying on the property, and all three of them were chasing each other around the one-third acre.

My parents were already sitting at the dining room table. We talked about everything that had transpired during our stay in Ukiah while we drank coffee. I called my in-laws in Ukiah to let them know we had made it safely. I needed to start looking for work immediately and asked my mother to save the job section of the paper for me for the next few days.

My father was upset that I had joined the Navy. He was a civilian employed by the Department of Defense. With an IQ equivalent to Albert Einstein and a degree in astrophysics from MIT, he designed lasers and defensive weapon systems for the Navy.

He told me that he had known many enlisted men over the decades, and their pay scale made it difficult to make ends meet for almost everyone he had known. He commented that when I was working as a project manager in Beverly Hills and Malibu, I was making more money than he did after thirty-five years at his job. He wondered aloud how was I going to support my family on a tiny fraction of what I was used to making. I told him that my bigger opportunities would come after I did my six-year tour of duty, and I would try to set aside some money before I left from whatever work I could find during the next five months.

My first thought was to call the company I had left about eight months ago, but there were two problems with that. First, the general contractor was upset when I had declined his offer of a generous salary and half ownership in the company; second, I'd be leaving in five months. I decided it was probably not a good idea to pursue that avenue.

My father had emphysema and was not that mobile anymore, so there were always projects that needed to be done around the house. With fruit trees and over 5,000 square feet of lawn, my mother, a retired schoolteacher, was always working in the yard. In addition to job hunting, I occupied my time helping around the house for the first several weeks after we arrived.

My son really enjoyed being at his grandparents' home. Ventura County was much warmer than Ukiah or even the Central Coast, and the beach was only fifteen to twenty minutes away. The entire family and many friends came to a big party for our son's third birthday.

My wife began to look for work as a waitress at the many local establishments. I told her there was only one place she shouldn't apply—a restaurant that had become the biggest cocaine hangout in town soon after it opened in the late 1970s. I didn't want her anywhere near that place, but she filled out employment applications at restaurants within a twenty-mile radius over the next several days.

Within a few weeks, she had an almost full-time waitress job, but she didn't tell me where she was working. When she claimed she was making huge tips but never had any money, I found out a few weeks later that she was working at the only place I had forbidden her to work. Then I knew where all her money was going, and I was angry. My wife had broken all her promises again and was back into cocaine.

She began coming home extremely late at night or not at all. My father would confront me because he would see her sitting in her car at 2:00 in the morning, smoking pot to come down from the coke. My father did not want her in his house anymore and told her so to her face. Though he said my son and I could stay, she had to go. My youngest brother and his wife lived in an apartment in the next town, and they invited us to stay with them until I could find work. Once we moved in with them, we rarely saw my wife. Her life was all about partying again.

The rumors and stories made me sick. Friends of my siblings that still lived locally would tell me about her activities at the restaurant. She would take off her wedding ring and tell people she was my brother's sister, not married to the oldest brother. It was a stupid thing to do because everyone around knew our family well. It soon became widely known that she was spending nights and weekends in motels and hotels near the restaurant with locally known drug kingpins.

At that point, I determined I would never take her back again. I finally admitted that I had made the worst possible choice when I married her and realized she would never change. It made me sick to hear her name because it just reminded me of everything I had forgiven her for when we had reconciled so many times before. She had little or no concern for our son, rarely ever seeing him or spending time with him. She was too busy having her own brand of fun.

About the same time, I met my brother's friend who lived in the same apartment complex. He was a painting contractor and knew that I was a carpenter. He told me a carpenter where he worked had quit that day and said he would talk to the job superintendent for me.

The next day, he brought over some beers and told me to show up at the job at 8:00 the next morning. He had scheduled an interview for me. I was both relieved and excited about the possibility of a good job. He told me there was almost a year left on the project, and that it was a great company that worked big projects throughout the state. I decided that I would say nothing about joining the Navy in May if I got the job. I would just wait and give a two-week notice before I shipped out.

The job site was located just down the hill from my parents' home. I arrived promptly at 8:00 a.m. at the job trailer that morning and introduced myself. I had my briefcase in hand and filled out an application while the superintendent was on the phone.

When our interview began and he asked about my experience, I pulled out a copy of the *Better Homes and Gardens Architect Edition*. I showed him the kitchen I had built for the famous Beverly Hills producer. I described my work as a project manager for the construction company and let him know I was well versed in every construction trade. He said I was overqualified for the job that they had and that I probably made a lot more money than he did. I told him I really needed the job as I was a single parent going through a divorce. I let him know I had just moved my family down from northern California because I couldn't find any work. He hired me that day for a one-week probationary period. He walked me through the various units being remodeled and told me what he expected to see accomplished in one week. He also introduced me to the lead carpenter that I would be working with on some of the tasks. I was told to roll out my tools and be ready to start at 7:00 a.m. the next day. The crews worked until 3:30 p.m., but rolling up tools was done on your own time.

I drove up to my parents' house to tell them that I had just found a really good job, but before I could ask to move back into their home to be closer to the job site, they had already requested that we return—so my son and I moved back in.

My wife had reopened the divorce case up in San Luis Obispo County, and I had to travel there on several occasions for shared custody mediation. She was trying to get child support and welfare to subsidize her partying. We arranged joint custody, and the split was almost fifty-fifty.

Once her paperwork and benefits were established, she dropped off our son at my parents' and would pick him up only on the day she collected her welfare. I just documented everything with the Sheriff's Department every time she refused to take her assigned custody, even though I didn't want our son with her. So many events happened during this period of time that I believed our son wasn't safe in her care. In light of this, my upcoming military service was a problem. I called my recruiters in Santa Rosa and told them what was happening.

As things got worse with my ex-wife, I called them about once a week asking them to make an appointment for me to talk with Command. I needed to be released from my military duty obligation. They always told me they would see what they could do, but they rarely returned my calls. Everybody made it a point of telling me that once you were sworn in to military service, nobody was released from duty unless you were dead.

Work was going well, and I was making a lot of good friends along the way. Some of the subcontractors even offered me work after the current project was complete. Working for that company was like being part of a close-knit family, but only a handful of trusted co-workers knew I had to ship out for the Navy in May.

I spent a lot of time with my three-year-old son. I even took him down to Sea World in San Diego several times. He loved the seals, dolphins, and killer whales. I was surprised at the attention I received from women as a single dad with a young son, but a girlfriend was the last thing I needed.

As May approached, I called my recruiters more often. They recommended that it would be better to ship out to "A" school in Chicago and arrange a meeting with Command there. I felt that once in Chicago, my chances of being released were slim to none. One of my recruiters was worried that I might decide to just go AWOL, but they were tired of hearing from me. I kept expressing how bad the situation was with my ex-wife, but I tried to leave out any discussion of drug use or addiction as I was extremely embarrassed about this and I felt it reflected badly upon me. Although the recruiters told me they were doing everything in their power to arrange a meeting with command, my feeling was that they were just buying time until I had to ship out. I became more insistent in my phone calls that were being made every couple of days.

Finally, one of the recruiters told me that he had contacted superiors that he had personal ties to and had managed to arrange an appointment with Command. He told me I needed to be in the same MEPS center in Oakland at 7:00 a.m. the morning I was to scheduled to ship out of Los Angeles. He told me that if I was late, I was going to Leavenworth Prison and he was in big trouble too. He seemed to be sincere, but maybe they were all just tired of my repeated calls to their office.

My father and I spoke at length several times on the subject of shipping out. He knew I would not go AWOL, but he urged me to just ship out. He had never heard of anyone being released from duty without severe penalties. Many of his brothers and other relatives had done military service in the past. He even consulted them on the subject and shared their input, which was to ship out and to never, ever go AWOL. All those he talked to told my father that I would never be allowed to see any Command personnel.

My personal feelings were that I had just over a fifty percent chance of getting out of the Navy. I felt I must try for the future and welfare of my young son. I would talk to many good friends after work. Many on the construction crew had done military service at one time or another in their lives. All them told me the same thing—that it was impossible to get out after being sworn in, and I just had to suck it up and ship out.

It was mid April 1991. Time was running out. I went into the job trailer, a little over two weeks before my date of departure and told the superintendent that I would be joining the Navy in May. I also apologized for not being forthcoming with this information when I was hired.

I was slated to be in Oakland at 7:00 a.m. on a Friday morning, so I called my ex-wife to make arrangements to leave our son with her. I told her that once I was collecting a salary, I would send her what I could to help support our child. Our son had been with me almost all of the last five months. She enjoyed her freedom and partying lifestyle, and I hurt inside because she was in no shape to be responsible for or to parent our son. But there was nothing I could do, either legally or physically.

About that time, a close family friend came to visit my parents. The woman, a nun, was my godmother's sister from Hawaii, and she was about the same age as my mother. She had watched my siblings and me grow up over the years, but I hadn't seen her in well over a decade. Although she was not my aunt by relation, we called her "Auntie."

One afternoon, about ten days before I was to ship out, Auntie overheard a heated exchange on the phone between me and my ex-wife. When I hung up, she calmly confronted me.

"I have heard from family members about what you are going through. I see the hurt in your eyes. We have to sit down and talk; there are many things I need to tell you. This is one of the reasons I am here." So we sat on the couch in the family room as she started, "Please tell me what is going on."

I talked for a half hour about some of the problems in my marriage and all the times I had reconciled with my wife. I spoke, sometimes with tears in my eyes, of my worries and concerns for the welfare and safety of my son.

When I was done, Auntie began, "I have known you since you were a very small child. God is watching over you and wants you to have custody of your son. Others tell me you are planning to try to get out of the Navy, but they believe you will not be successful. You have a plan; you have a good plan. You must follow through with this plan and stay strong. Do not listen to others; they are not you. You will succeed if you first believe in yourself. You are who you are, and you have done many things that people consider impossible. You must continue to succeed. You must set an example for others, and many will learn and change as a result of your efforts and actions."

Our conversation continued for over an hour. She did most of the talking. She talked about what she had seen in my life since I was young and God's plan for me; she drew an analogy between me and Michael the Archangel due to the way I would stand up and fight for others. Many of the things she talked about were very, very deep. Auntie returned to Hawaii about a week before my scheduled departure, but our conversation affected me deeply and positively. The things she said that day made me feel empowered and self-assured—I even felt my chances of being successful in arguing my case for release to Military Command might be more like eighty-five to ninety-five percent.

CHAPTER 13

OAKLAND BOUND

I relinquished my son to the custody of my wife a few days before I was to leave. She was living in Ventura, in an apartment shared with a drug dealer/businessman and other women. For the last five months, he had been with me all except the one day a month when my wife would take him with her to the welfare department and claim that she had sole custody and that I refused to give her child support. Then she collected her welfare check for party money and returned our son to me that same day. This had been her established pattern since our last separation, but I had no other legal choice for his care since I might still have to enter the military.

I woke up the Thursday morning before my reporting date feeling a bit indecisive. No one had ever been released from military duty after being sworn in—at least, not without severe penalties. But the urgency I felt about getting custody of my three-year-old son instantly canceled out any second thoughts I had of not following through with my plan.

I drank several cups of coffee, hopped into my truck and headed down to the auto parts store. I had at least seven hours of driving ahead of me that night and figured I would depart the family home in Ventura County around 11:00 p.m. that night. I picked up five quarts of Castrol oil and a Fram oil filter.

Upon returning home, I changed the oil and checked all the fluids, including transmission and differential fluids, in my truck. I jacked it up and removed the wheels and rear brake drums to check brake wear. I did a visual check on the front brake pads and calipers. I had been meticulous about maintaining my vehicles since I was a teenager, and many of my friends referred to me as a master mechanic.

Next, I decided to vacuum the interior and wash the truck. It looked as new as the day I bought it when I was done. If I ended up shipping out or going to military prison tomorrow, I would call my brother in Livermore, which was not too far east of Oakland. He would sell my truck, pay off the few remaining payments and get the balance of the money to my parents to hold for my son's needs.

Around lunchtime, I decided it would be a good idea to take a nap in preparation for the long drive. I slept for a couple of hours and made my final preparations for the trip when I woke up. My briefcase was organized with divorce papers, a letter I had prepared for the court, and over fifty handwritten diary pages that I had been keeping for almost a year to document my wife's behavior and activities. I also had police reports pertaining to the numerous times she had violated custody orders, the time she ran over me with her car at childcare, etc. I would need these official reports later when I challenged the court's orders regarding custody. They legally documented incidents showing her pattern of using our son only to collect money from welfare, but I felt they would also help my case with Military Command. Finally, I packed my case of cassette tapes and my cell phone. I would definitely need music on the monotonous sections of Interstate 5 in the Central Valley of California.

My truck was completely ready for my road trip. I planned to drive all night, stopping only for one tank of gas and coffee. The rest areas along Interstate 5 would provide places to stretch my legs and use the restroom when I needed a break.

Our family had dinner in the early evening. Towards the end of the meal, my father asked, "How are you getting Los Angeles International Airport tomorrow morning? Do you need us to drive you?"

I answered with, "Dad, you know what my plans are. I am not going to change them. My appointment with Command is at 7:00 a.m. at the Oakland MEPS center where I was inducted. I don't want to discuss this any further. I am leaving tonight before midnight. The welfare and future of my son, your first grandchild, depends on my actions tomorrow. I know you think it will be impossible, but I have hopes that Command will at least hear what I have to say before shipping me out to 'A' school or sending me to Leavenworth."

Everyone at the table was silent, and my father backed down from pushing points he had made in our discussions over the last few weeks. My mother made a fresh pot of coffee after dinner for my trip. Later on, I hugged my family as I prepared to get on the road. Two thermos bottles of coffee in hand, I headed out the garage door to my truck. I laid out three or four cassette tapes on the truck seat and selected the "Best of the Doobie Brothers" to start out the drive.

I wove down the hill to Highway 118. This would take me past Moorpark where I had attended junior college for a few semesters. From there, I would continue east toward Magic Mountain Amusement Park then travel several hours north on Interstate 5 before connecting with one of the highways that would take me westward into Oakland and the Bay Area.

As I passed Magic Mountain and headed north on I-5, I turned off the stereo so I could listen to my truck's motor and make sure nothing sounded out of the ordinary. I had driven the truck over 130,000 miles in the last two years. Some weeks, while working in the Los Angeles area, I drove well over 1,200 miles between jobs and home on the central California coast.

The 3.9 liter V6 motor in my 1987 Dakota powered up the Grapevine grade as if it were a V8. That's when I thought about the V8 Dodge Dakota I had taken for a test drive a couple of weeks prior. I had visited the Dodge dealer in Ventura to inquire about the cost to fix my transmission—the reverse gear synchromesh was going out, so I had to physically hold the gearshift in reverse. One of the salesmen showed me a brand new 4WD, 5.2 liter V8, Extra Cab they had on the lot. That truck was selling for about $20,000 and had some buyer incentives for previous Dodge truck owners. We took a long test drive and afterwards that salesman was sure he had a sale—until I told him I was scheduled to ship out for the Navy in two weeks. Then I told him I'd be back to buy the truck if I could get out of the Navy and get my old job back.

He replied with a skeptical laugh, "Yeah, right." From his point of view, I had wasted his time, and he was bummed.

Once I was down the north side of the Grapevine grade, I set the cruise control at eighty miles per hour for those long, straight sections of I-5 and poured a fresh cup of hot coffee. I would occasionally tap the cruise control up around 90 miles per hour to shave some time off my trip because I anticipated hitting heavy traffic around Oakland at dawn. I was under the impression that my recruiters had gone out of their way and pulled some strings to arrange my appointment with Command, and I could not be late for this meeting.

I had always been able to do my best thinking while driving, and this trip was no exception. I thought about all the things I wanted to say during my appointment with Command. I also thought about the possibility that my recruiters had lied to me about actually arranging a meeting with Command. I prepared myself by imagining the worst-case scenario of what might happen. I then considered the best-case scenario since I needed to be prepared for any possible outcome. If I were to back down and just ship out as everybody said I should, I would never consider myself to be worthy of parenting my child. My bottom line was that his future was far more important than mine. In my opinion, people who do not have children rarely reach this level of commitment, and parents who do not have this level of commitment should not be parents to begin with.

As I got close to Oakland, I realized that traffic was heavier than I had expected. I exited the highway into downtown Oakland and immediately started looking for a parking lot or parking structure. I found one east of downtown that seemed reasonable and located one open spot on the fourth level, but I was behind my projected schedule and realized that I was going to be late for my appointment.

CHAPTER 14

ALL OR NOTHING

I locked the truck and made sure the hidden spare key was still there, in case my brother had to come retrieve my truck. I headed for the stairway leading out of the parking garage, hoping to get a view of Oakland's skyline so I could get a bearing on where I was headed. I believed I was within a six-block radius of the MEPS facility.

Briefcase in hand, I hit the surface streets heading west at a fast stride. It was after 7:00 a.m. now, so I was officially late. I looked for anything familiar, relying on my instinct to guide me. I felt confident I could find the MEPS, but I also decided that if I hadn't located the facility in half an hour, I would return to the truck and call the recruiting office in Santa Rosa when they opened so they could give me directions.

Walking on the north side of the street, I noticed a building that looked familiar across the street about 200 feet ahead. As I got closer, I realized it was definitely the place where I had spent the night after taking the ASVAP. I looked down the street to my immediate right and it seemed surprisingly familiar as I recalled running alongside the bus... I remembered that the driver made a left turn just after letting me board the bus that morning, five months ago.

That meant the street on my immediate right probably led to the rear of the MEPS, so I turned right on the next street to look for the front entrance to the building. I began to jog and then run as I saw a familiar concrete stairway and steel handrail traveling up the center, close to the end of the city block. I was sure I had found the front entrance to the MEPS center.

Reaching the top of the stairs, I paused for a deep breath. The thought of "Here goes something" flashed through my head. I could see that lights were on inside the building through scratches in the blacked out windows. I pulled open the door and stepped into the well-lit lobby.

I noticed two guards with shouldered rifles to the right of the entrance. I turned towards a counter to my right. As the guards saw me, their rifles rolled off their shoulders. Three other MPs were in motion towards me from other locations in the lobby.

One MP shouted loudly, "ON THE FLOOR! NOW! LOSE THE BRIEFCASE!"

By the time I was face down on the floor, all five guards were upon me with their rifles trained on me. One MP kicked my briefcase about five feet away from my body.

One guard demanded, "Identify yourself. What are you doing here?"

I replied with my full name and told him that I had an appointment scheduled with Command of this base, made by my recruiters.

He replied, "Nobody gets an appointment with Command of this base! We'll see about this." He walked back to the wall phone by his station near the front door.

As he spoke on the phone, another MP said, "What's in the briefcase? Give me the combination."

I told him that my briefcase was not locked and it contained legal paperwork pertinent to the reasons for my appointment with Command. He began searching through my briefcase. While I was talking, another MP was patting me down for weapons. There were at least two rifles on me at all times.

The MP searching my briefcase said, "His briefcase is clear." As the other guard returned from the phone he began, "Mr. K, you were listed as AWOL (Absent Without Leave) from Los Angeles International Airport twenty-five minutes ago. I would say that you are on your way to prison, except for the fact that you are present in a military installation. I can't believe that you believed the bullshit those recruiters fed you. Like I said, nobody gets an appointment with Command. Remain still; someone from upstairs is on the way down."

There was a loud ding as the elevator across the lobby arrived on the floor. As the doors opened, I saw a red-haired, red-mustached officer with glasses standing alone. He was shorter than I am, and his build was slightly smaller than mine.

As the officer stepped from the elevator, he ordered, "Get him up off the floor!"

Two MPs grabbed my arms and quickly lifted me to face the red-haired officer.

I stood at attention as another MP asked, "What about the briefcase, sir?"

The officer replied, "Give it to him. Side your firearms, men. I will take care of this. Follow me, Mr. K."

As I followed him towards the elevator, two guards started to follow behind me. The officer stopped before entering the elevator. He turned toward the MPs saying, "I don't believe your presence will be necessary, men. Do we need armed guards, Mr. K?"

"No, sir," I replied. "Thank you, sir."

The officer and I entered the elevator as he ordered the guards to return to their stations. The elevator trip was completed in silence as we traveled up several floors. I followed him out of the elevator and into a nicely organized office that was obviously his. He ordered me to have a seat and said, "You have a lot of explaining to do." Then he continued, "Who made you believe that you had an appointment with Command of this base? This base is secret; how did you find it? What did you think you were going to accomplish by showing up here today? What makes you think anyone here is going to listen to anything you have to say? I don't care if you are the 'Son of Superman,' you have sworn an oath to this country and you are expected to honor that oath. No one is released from duty after being sworn in. NEVER! You now have the floor; I expected full and complete answers."

For the next fifteen to twenty minutes, I gave a brief synopsis of the events that had transpired over the last five months and then elaborated on my conversations and frequency of calls to the recruiters in Santa Rosa, California. I ended with, "Sir, I joined the Navy to serve my country because we were at war. Operation Desert Storm went off surgically with almost no opposition. This country does not need my services now, but my son does."

He countered by explaining that personnel with my qualifications were hard to find. He elaborated that only a very small group of enlistees had the intelligence and psychological balance required to be given the responsibility of launching nuclear weapons.

Changing the subject back to one of his primary questions, I then explained at length everything that I had remembered from five months ago about the MEPS facility and its location. I told him how I had recognized the overnight accommodations just down the street, and from that, I was able to determine the base's location.

He thanked me for explaining and was relieved that my recruiters hadn't given me the location of the base. While he was angry that the recruiters had told me I had an appointment with Command, he did comment that many recruiters would probably have done something similar—never believing that any new enlistee would "have the balls" to show up at Command Headquarters instead of shipping out.

I asked the officer if I could show him the legal papers and documents I had in my briefcase.

He replied shortly, "No one here has any interest in any of the crap you have in that briefcase. The only issue here today is whether you are shipping out to your 'A' school or going to military prison."

I attempted to interject a few words, "Sir, the future and welfare of my son hang in the balance based on what happens here today."

He interrupted me with, "It couldn't be that bad, even though you believe it is. Divorces and custody issues are nothing new. You just need to ship out today and let the Navy's attorneys help you make your case to the courts and get custody of your son."

It was now or never. I began with, "Sir, with all due respect, is the United States Navy prepared to give me that guarantee in writing? No, they are not. I have signed up for six years deployment, and no court will see fit to give a parent custody who might be stationed and moved more than a dozen times during the next six years. The ages of three to eight are the most formative years for any child, and I fear that the consequences of my wife's lifestyle will be a serious threat to the safety and welfare of my son."

Once again he interrupted with, "Stop right there. I do not have time for this. Come with me; you will be given the opportunity to talk to someone else about this."

I followed him out of his office and down the hallway to another office. Once again I was told to take a seat and "listen well." From the documents framed on the office walls, I gathered that this officer had a degree in psychology and was probably a psychiatrist.

He began his speech. "Mr. K, you have been sworn into the U.S. Military and taken an Oath of Service. You are legally bound to this contract. Refusal to honor this contract is considered desertion, and you will go to military prison for fifteen years. Right now it is in your best interests to voluntarily ship to your 'A' school in Chicago. This is also in the best interests of your son. Your job choice of Fire Control of Nuclear Weapons is highly respected. You do realize that to be cleared for such a job requires not only the most intelligent of all enlistees but the most psychologically balanced individuals ever tested. Right now, you are making some of us question your psychological balance and qualifications for your selected job assignment. I want you to take some time and think very carefully about your course of action today before you respond any further."

I saw this as my only chance to make my points. I felt it best to show no hesitation in the direction I intended to take. I instantly responded, "Sir, may I have the floor?"

Though seemingly surprised that I had spoken so quickly, he nodded.

I continued and the words just flowed unrehearsed. "I have spent weeks and months thinking this through to the nth degree. I am quite prepared to go to prison over this matter as I will be of no beneficial service to this country if I am worried about the safety of my young son. If I ship out to 'A' school today, it will be at gunpoint, sir. Yes, I have taken an oath to this country and government, and its citizens. Yes, I do realize that going against this constitutes desertion. However, sir, my obligation to my child as a parent outweighs any obligation to any other human being, country, or government. My obligation to my child outweighs my obligation to God himself, if I may be so forward."

My tone and my words seemed to surprise him. The officer asked me to elaborate on what had been going on at home. I spoke for about thirty minutes, describing my wife's patterns of behavior and neglect of our son. I told how she continued to prioritize partying and drug use over parenting. I offered to show him police reports and documentation to back my claims, but he also declined to see anything in my briefcase.

The officer and I went back and forth for another half hour. I countered every point he made with an instant response that showed my obvious commitment to my child. He offered the opinion that I was under undue stress over recent incidents and perhaps I should alter my approach and ask for a few months' delay before shipping out. I countered by pointing out that my choice to enlist could be viewed as being initiated by undue stress—exactly the opposite of points he was making.

Others would have probably been convinced to reconsider their position based on his arguments, but he realized that wasn't going to happen with me. He paused, picked up the phone on his desk, and spoke to someone briefly. After hanging up, he asked me to follow as he escorted me to another office.

I was once again seated in front of another psychiatrist. This man was a bit older, balding slightly, with brown hair and glasses. He opened by making the same basic points, but he talked more about the consequences I would face if I were to continue to refuse to ship out. He, too, suggested that I seek a delay in my ship date. I repeated my arguments again and elaborated even more on the circumstances that led to my initial enlistment. He realized that he was making no headway with me. After an hour or so, he too called someone then escorted me to another office.

As I sat before the fourth officer, obviously another psychiatrist, he said simply "This is your last chance to ship out voluntarily. Are you really willing to sit in prison for fifteen years? What good is that going to do for your son?"

I replied, "Yes, I am, sir." I stood up and put my wrists forward towards him as if to be handcuffed. I once again repeated the same statement I had made earlier, that my obligation as a parent to the safety and welfare of my son outweighed my obligation to anyone else.

A bit shocked at my response, he picked up his phone and said, "Get him out of here; this is futile."

Through the door stepped the original red-haired officer, the first man who had met me in the lobby, a few hours earlier. He was accompanied by an armed MP and said, "Come with me, Mr. K."

We wove our way through several hallways, me following the officer and the guard on my heels. Finally, a steel door was held open for me. The small room had a concrete bench, very similar to a temporary holding cell or drunk tank in a jail. I had entered the brig.

As I stepped inside, the guard asked, "What about the briefcase, sir?"

The officer responded, "We'll let him keep it for now."

I took a seat on the cold concrete bench. As the door slammed shut, I looked through the small double-thickness security glass of the door to see the guard take position outside the door with his rifle in front of him. I also noticed video cameras at either end of the cell, similar to the ones I had seen in every office and hallway I had been in since arriving.

About three hours passed. I tried to take a nap because I had been driving all night, but I couldn't get comfortable. I was still wired from all the coffee as well as the adrenaline from the events and conversations of the morning. I passed the time by reviewing the contents of my briefcase. I read and re-read the dozens of pages I had written for the courts. I read over police reports of incidents with my wife. I considered that these were probably my last hours as a free man.

I closed my eyes to rest them as I mulled over points I had not discussed with any of the officers I had spoken with. Some could be taken as egotistical, so I would bring them up only as a last resort—but I was ready to say, "Look at the incredible contributions I have already made to this country and the medical community. I have, by accident, exposed a severe flaw in the NORAD Defense System of the United States of America. No security expert or software engineer did this; I did. I have supplied top doctors and genetic researchers with a DNA sample that they claim is advanced 1,000 years ahead of the human race. I have completely reset the benchmarks for human intelligence and abilities. No monetary compensation can or will be made for the things I have already contributed. Though I will never be given recognition for any of these things, I am not just your average enlistee, or your average human being for that matter ... "

Focusing on these thoughts pumped me up, and I also felt more relaxed as I knew I could give these arguments as a last resort. I was confident that Command would give me one more chance to change my mind or argue my case to be released. I had to be ready to throw everything I had at them, for my son's future was depending on it.

Becoming impatient was pointless. My assumption was that while I was in the brig, transportation was being arranged to military prison, but I felt they might offer me one last chance to ship out voluntarily. I was committed to standing my ground and not changing my position. I needed to be released from duty in order to be able to have any chance of getting custody of my son through the California court system.

CHAPTER 15

COMMAND'S DECISION

I could tell it was early afternoon without looking at my watch. After all, I had been awake for about twenty-four hours. The time I had spent with my eyes closed seemed to make me feel rested although my mind was continually processing every possible scenario and outcome. I felt I had covered all the possibilities, and I was ready to accept the worst.

I heard talking outside the steel door and the sound of a key in the lockset. The guard stepped aside as the door opened and there stood the red-haired officer again.

"Come with me, Mr. K," he said as he motioned with his hand.

I followed him through the hallways with the armed MP on my heels again. We once again arrived at his office and entered. The guard took his position outside the door and closed it.

"Have a seat," the officer requested as he sat back in his chair. He followed again with the question from earlier that morning, "What did you hope to accomplish here today?"

I began, "Sir, I believe I have accomplished my goal. I only wanted Command to hear what I had to say in regards to the safety and welfare of my child. You and several others have patiently listened to what I have had to say, and I am thankful to each and every one of you for taking the time to listen and to talk to me."

I continued, "Sir, not to be redundant, but I feel that it is imperative to the future of my son that I be released from my service obligation to this country. There is no way that the courts of the State of California will see fit to award custody to a single parent currently on active duty—especially one who has made a six-year commitment. It is not that I want to get out of military duty; it's just that this is the only way I will have a chance of being awarded custody."

There was a long pause before he spoke. "Mr. K, the Commander of this base and I have been on the phone with the President and our superiors all the way up the chain of command for the Department of Defense while you have been sitting in the brig. You have created quite a problem and embarrassment to us here today."

He took a deep breath and briefly paused before saying, "At this point, I would like to say something off the record, and of a more personal nature. I am a father myself of two young daughters. I would hope that if I were in the same position you are in, I would show the same devotion and commitment that you have exhibited here today. Many of us today are impressed with your show of resolve and determination. This, however, does not affect the decision that has been made."

As he looked me up and down, he continued, "The President has more important things to do than decide what will happen to you here today. He does not want to make that decision. He has left that decision up to the Commander of this base. The Commander of this base does not want to see you, listen to you, or even acknowledge you. He is extremely embarrassed that this incident has taken place on his watch and on his base. He has left the decision up to his second in command."

The officer turned in his swivel chair and picked up a manila envelope from a table behind him. He removed a stack of papers over a half inch thick from the packet. He stood and placed the papers facing me and flipped about ten pages in. On that page there were two columns of names filling the entire page.

He then said, "I want you to look at the names on this page and tell me how many names you recognize. Do not point to any names. Do not say any names. Simply tell me the rough number of names on this page that are familiar."

On the first page, I told him that I recognized six to eight names. He flipped the page and I told him that I recognized about ten names. On the third page, I saw about a dozen names that I was familiar with.

I made the comment, "While I am acquainted with some of these names, most of them are friends and acquaintances of my wife. Some of them are her past employers and co-workers." After flipping through about eight pages, the officer said, "Well, I think that is enough. Do you know what this is, Mr. K?"

I replied with, "No, sir, I don't. What is it?"

"Mr. K, this is the Drug Enforcement Agency file on your wife. She has been under state and federal surveillance for about ten years before you even met her. In every place she has lived, she has become involved with known drug dealers and made her way to the top individuals. She is not a federal agent, but the DEA and others have used her like a bloodhound to expose narcotic traffickers. Well, that is up until about the time she met you. As you have tried to tell us today, she is back to her old ways. You do have serious problems as far as your son's welfare and safety are concerned. This file substantiates your claims and proves that you are not bullshitting us. This file is considered classified. We would not normally have access to these documents except for the permissions granted by those in the highest positions today. Technically, you never saw this file. This file is no reflection on you or your son. This file concerns only your wife. Officially, this file does not exist."

I was shocked and severely embarrassed. The only reply I could come up with was, "Sir, I am incredibly embarrassed and ashamed of this. You have confirmed the suspicions I've had for a long time. Although it hurts me to say this, I want to thank you and this government's agencies for sharing this with me."

I took a long, deep breath as he paused. There was an extended period of silence as he returned the file to its envelope and tossed it back onto the table behind him.

He rotated his chair to face me and broke the silence with, "This morning when you met me, you probably thought that I was just another officer of this installation, but I am second in command of this military base. Since I have spent the most time with you today, it is up to me to decide your fate. This has not been easy. I have spent hours thinking this through. My decision is final and official. I choose to attrite you."

I said without expression, "I'm sorry, sir, but I am not sure what the word attrite means."

His eyes lit up as he replied loudly, "Aha! One point for me! I know something the Son of Superman doesn't know!" His jubilance faded, and he said seriously, "Attrite means to be released without penalty, Mr. K. Now you can add that to your list of unmatched accomplishments. You are now the first and only man to ever be released from military duty without penalty. You are the only one to ever successfully argue such a case, and the only one ever allowed to do so. This is the first and only time this will ever happen, but there are some non-negotiable conditions that accompany this decision. We will get to those in a few minutes. Right now, I would like to get your take on all of this."

"Sir? I mean, thank you, sir! I am so grateful to all of you," I answered.

He continued, "You come in here as an enlistee five months ago and blow everyone's mind. You put this country at DEFCON 4. The President flies to meet you in the middle of the night and is then denied that meeting by the Secret Service after you managed to escape past a dozen armed guards and undercover agents. You display an incredible base of knowledge and expertise, not to mention the things you can do that humans aren't supposed to be able to do. Now, this morning, you get listed as AWOL over 500 miles away, walk in the front door of a secret military base, and successfully present a case to be released. What is your view on all that has happened?"

The only words that entered my mind were, "Well, sir, the only thing I can say is that it becomes obvious to me that there are higher powers at work in this universe and these things are just meant to be. I myself believe that there are actually no accidents in life."

He smiled and replied, "That's pretty much my thoughts on the subject and the same thing many of my superiors have said today."

I was relieved to say the least. I could feel the tension release through my whole body. Tears of happiness started to well up in my eyes, but I knew we were far from being finished. I had to maintain my composure.

He picked up another manila envelope from his desk and started the second part of our conference with, "I have been cleared and asked to present you with the following:

"We, at the Department of Defense, would like you to reconsider your decision. We are willing to give you whatever time you need to get custody of your son and return to service. It is now my turn to blow your mind, Mr. K. The entire Chain of Command of the Department of Defense unanimously feels that you should be groomed for the Presidency. We feel that no human being has ever lived who is more qualified to be the president of the United States and leader of the free world."

He was right; I was shocked by his statement, and I listened carefully as he continued.

"In this envelope are your formal attrition papers with official stamps and signatures. If anyone should ever question your release from service, you are to show them this first page. Officially, the reason for attrition will be listed as 'Refusal to Ship.' This is not an acceptable reason. We have done this to avoid mountains of paperwork being added to the mountains that you have already created. Many of us consider some of the points you have made here today to be unarguable. Heck, the statement 'Who has the ability or is qualified to argue against the Son of Superman' was made by more than one of my superiors today.

"The second page in this envelope contains a bar code. If at any time before your thirty-fourth birthday, you wish to join the United States Military, you are to present the bar code on this piece of paper to any recruiting office or any military base. You will be flown immediately and directly to Washington D.C. to meet the President and his Cabinet in the White House before being shipped to your 'A' school. Upon completion of 'A' school, you will go directly to Officer's Training School. We are completely serious; we want you to be the president of the United States."

I was not expecting any of this. I had mentally prepared myself for going to military prison for fifteen years, and instead I was being offered the presidency.

My words flowed naturally as I responded, "Sir, I am so appreciative of the decisions made today on behalf of my son and myself. I am especially appreciative and even shocked by the vote of confidence the Department of Defense has given me.

"At this point in time, my only concern is the future and welfare of my child, and that must remain my first priority. As far as the presidency goes, well, sir, I am not an angel. With all the mudslinging that accompanies politics, someone will dig up some kind of trash that could undermine even the best efforts to put me in office. In other words, sir, to put it another way, I do not believe in politics."

To this he replied, "Mr. K, everyone has something they are not proud of in their past. We have already vetted you extensively before even considering or telling you any of this. The government has ways of making 'unbecoming' things disappear, if you know what I mean. You can set aside any thoughts of anything you may think you have in your past that would detract from your ability to seek office."

"Well, sir, while I am honored to be held in this respect, I feel that I will be as great an asset to this country and its citizens in civilian life as in the Navy. I do not, and will not ever, accept corruption and other issues that are not in the best interests of the American people. While I do not consider myself to be worthy of the presidency, I will raise leaders."

Little did I know at that point in time that I was foreshadowing my own future. Ten years later I would be blackmailed by an attorney being vetted as a federal superior court judge and members of the District Attorney's office in a mountain community of California. It was my phone call in the early 2000s to a California senator that prompted same day emergency legislation to fund the then-defunct California Bar Association. The following morning, disciplinary action was started against all the individuals involved.

"Well, we have no doubts about that, but we must now discuss the conditions of your release," the officer said in a serious voice.

After a short pause he continued, "In doing our jobs, protecting national security and the citizens of this country, we must consider you to be one of two extremes. Because of your abilities, you must first be considered the most dangerous enemy and weapon this country could ever face. Hell, if someone pisses you off, not only does this country have a serious problem, but the human race is over.

"On the other hand, and more likely the case, you are considered the greatest asset to ever walk this planet. For these precautionary reasons, you are now the first human being ever to be put under periodic lifetime surveillance for a non-criminal reason by the Federal Bureau of Investigation, the Central Intelligence Agency, the National Security Agency, and the Department of Defense. This is an Executive Order directly from the President and agreed upon by all agency heads."

The thought of "Wow, how do I accept all this?" flashed through my head. This action sounded insanely extreme.

The officer continued, "Now, let me explain this to you. Nobody is going to follow you around twenty-four hours a day. But every so often, agencies will be checking up on you and the people you associate with. You are free to do anything you wish with no restrictions. Heck, no one cares if you do drugs or travel wherever you want. Our concerns are that you do not become involved or align yourself with terrorist organizations or individuals. On the other side of the coin, if a foreign power or country should attempt to coerce you to work for them by threatening harm to any member of your family or loved ones, we will be forced to intervene. Those people closest to you will be watched over as a precaution. If I were you, I would attempt to just ignore all of this. It would be easy for the average individual to become overly paranoid over this, but as we all know, you are far from average. We will not intrude on your life or the lives of those you associate with. Once again, this is only precautionary. We are only looking out for our and your best interests."

I thought for a moment before I spoke. "Sir, while this sounds very extreme, what other choice do I really have? I see the points you have made clearly and the fact that I must accept this action by the government and its institutions."

He then said, "There is one final point to be made. You are not being, and will not ever be, asked to sign a statement of non-disclosure with this government or any of its institutions.

You are free to tell anyone anything that has happened here. The fact is, most people would think you are crazy. This country leaves the disclosure of your abilities to the world up to you; after all, this is who you are, and we have no right to tell you what you can and can not do."

This was an incredible amount of information for me to process all at once. I thanked the officer for all the time he had taken with me and especially the decisions made which would benefit my child custody case.

He then asked me if I was hungry and apologized that I was never offered lunch while I was under arrest and in the brig.

He offered, "We could go downstairs and order anything you want; the food is very good here, and lunch is on the Department of Defense ... but then again, you probably just want to get out of here and get back to your son and civilian life. Do you have any questions before you leave?"

To this I replied, "Thank you so very much for the offer, sir. I do have at least an eight- to ten-hour drive ahead of me now." He extended his hand to shake mine and said, "Well then, Mr. K, I offer you my congratulations on your successful day and wish you the best of luck in getting custody of your son. Please consider all I have said today over the next few months. I personally believe that you will be awarded custody in the near future."

"Thank you, sir," I replied.

He then escorted me out of his office and down the hall to the elevator. As the doors opened, he said, "You don't mind if I don't escort you down, do you? I have considerable paperwork to do now."

"No, sir, and thank you once again for all you have done for me."

As the elevator doors closed, I exhaled in relief. I had succeeded in getting out of military service. It was now time to turn my focus to obtaining custody of my three-year-old son.

The doors opened on the lobby floor of the building with a loud ding. As I stepped out of the elevator, the same two MPs at the front door saw me.

Again, the one in charge shouted, "HALT! Where do you think you are going?" as their rifles rolled off their shoulders and took aim at me.

As I walked towards them I answered with, "I have been attrited, and my paperwork is here in this envelope."

"That's not good enough for me! I will need to call upstairs to verify this," the MP in charge replied as the other slightly lowered his rifle.

As the one guard walked to his station to get on the phone, I told the other that I had just left the office of the second in command of the base.

He responded with, "If that's the case, this will all be cleared up in a moment."

I could hear the MP on the phone saying repeatedly, "Yes, sir. I understand, sir."

As he hung up the phone, he turned to the other guard and said, "Side your weapon." He then leaned his own rifle against the wall below the telephone.

He walked towards me, extending his right hand to shake mine and said, "Congratulations, Son of Superman! You are the only person ever to walk out these front doors. Everyone that enters these front doors leaves through another exit."

The second MP had a surprised look on his face as he extended his hand to shake mine, saying, "So you're the guy everyone around here is still talking about! It's a pleasure to meet you, and sorry about the rough treatment this morning."

"Hey, you guys are just doing your job. I'm just glad none of you shot me this morning!" I said in jest.

Light laughter and smiles prevailed as they wished me good luck in getting custody of my son. They then escorted me to the door and one of them opened it for me. Both MPs even saluted me before I stepped out the door.

Upon exiting, I stopped at the top of the stairs to retrieve my sunglasses from my briefcase before heading to the parking garage about five blocks east. It was late afternoon, and I would probably hit considerable traffic on my way out of Oakland.

CHAPTER 16

HOME FREE

When I reached my truck in the parking structure, I plugged in my cell phone and called my brother in Livermore.

His first words were, "Where do I have to go to pick up your truck?"

I told him that I had been successful at getting released from military duty and would reach his apartment in about two hours. I asked if I could sleep on his couch for awhile before the long drive back to southern California since I had been awake for over twenty-four hours and had spent all day arguing my case to Command. I asked him to pick up a case of Heineken beer to celebrate, and he suggested ordering pizza after I arrived.

When I reached Livermore, my brother greeted me with a high five and wanted to know all the details. As we drank our first couple of beers, I gave him the short version of what had happened.

He then said, "You know, a few weeks ago, when you told me of your plans to try to get an appointment with Command, I reminded you that the dads of two of our schoolmates had served as commanders of Pt. Mugu Naval Air Station." I remembered our conversation well. My younger brother had asked me if I wanted him to contact the two men to see if they could be of assistance, but I had asked him not to do so. I didn't want to involve anyone else in my personal matters.

My brother then told me that he had contacted both men that week anyway, and their advice was to ship out and attempt to get an audience with Command after arriving at my "A" school. They had told him that there was no chance I'd be released from my military obligation as I had planned and that I could easily end up in military prison for my efforts. After talking with them, he decided not to give me their input because he didn't want their opinion to have a negative impact on what I was attempting to accomplish.

My brother's roommates arrived home from work shortly, and we ordered pizzas. I became very sleepy once I ate and fell asleep on the couch soon after one of his roommates put a movie in the VCR.

Shortly after midnight I awoke to find my brother asleep in his reclining chair, and I couldn't doze off again. My system was still in overdrive from the events of the last day or so. I woke my brother to tell him I was getting back on the road; I still had a lot to think about, and driving was good for that.

An hour and a half later, I pulled into a gas station to top off my gas tank and fill one of my thermos bottles with fresh, hot coffee. I checked the tire pressure and all my running lights on the truck. I got back on Interstate 5 headed south, down through the Central Valley. A cassette tape by the group "Kansas" went into the Alpine stereo to pump my blood flow until the fresh hot coffee kicked in. Once wide awake, a "Best of the Eagles" tape put my mind to fluid thought as the boring repetition of dotted highway lines rolled on like an endless video loop in front of my eyes.

A few hours later I had finished my coffee, then I caught myself falling asleep at the wheel two or three times and decided I had better stop somewhere and sleep. The next town with accommodations was quite a ways down the highway, so I looked for a suitable place to park and close my eyes for a while. It must have been about 4:30 a.m. when I pulled about seventy-five yards off the highway close to a barbed wire fence that bordered several acres of Central Valley farmland.

I slept soundly and awoke around 9:00 a.m. to the truck shaking in extremely high winds. It would take another three or four hours to reach Ventura County, but I was rested and ready to drive again. The traffic heading south towards Los Angeles was not bad for mid-morning on a Saturday. Hours later, I pulled up in front of the family home and parked in the street. It was a little after noon. My father was walking down the sidewalk to check the mailbox. He had been ill with emphysema since he retired and had his oxygen tank in tow. My mother was working in the front yard trimming some of the juniper bushes.

As I exited the truck and headed towards the driveway, my father shouted out, "What are you doing here? You are AWOL and a deserter! I am a retired employee of the United States Government and Department of Defense! YOU will not bring this crap upon this family!"

I shouted back, "I was released from duty without penalty! I have all the official paperwork here in my hand!" I turned towards my mother and said, "Mom, can I show you these documents?"

She approached as I removed the two sheets of paper from the manila envelope. I pointed out the official Department of Defense stamps and signatures. As she looked at the second page with the bar code, I told her I would explain that page to both of them later. I needed to get my father to calm down before something happened to him health-wise. I asked my mother to take the papers to my father and show him.

Thirty feet away, I stood alone in the street at the tailgate of my truck. I watched my father read the first page. He shouted in a calmer tone, "How the hell did you do this?" Since he had been a physicist designing defensive weapon systems for the Navy for thirty-five years, he easily recognized the letterhead and format of the first page. He then told me to come into the house and explain how I had managed to get released from duty.

Once we were all sitting at the dining room table, Dad commented that he had known dozens of enlisted men over the decades and what I claimed to have done was impossible. I spent about an hour telling my parents a shortened version of what had happened. When my parents asked me what the bar code was for, I told them that I had been given the opportunity to return to service anytime before my thirty-fourth birthday. I omitted the part about being offered the presidency. I hadn't told my parents anything about the DEFCON 4 incident or the President flying to meet me five months earlier, and I didn't bring it up now. In fact, twelve to fifteen years would pass before I told any family members or friends the whole story. I feel the psychological need for fame and notoriety are conditioned into most people by society, civilization, and their environment—but I have never lusted after them.

I was exhausted. I went to the bedroom my son and I had been sharing and slept for over sixteen hours. I awoke Sunday, mid morning, feeling rested but sluggish. I was a little amazed that I felt as well as I did after driving more than a thousand miles and spending all day at the MEPS station on Friday. While driving home, I had considered taking a couple of days to unwind and relax; but now that I was home, I felt the need to keep moving toward my goals. I spent that Sunday organizing a plan in my head for the next few weeks, and the first thing on my agenda was to try to get my construction job back.

Monday morning I drove into the 450-unit housing complex where I had been working for the last few months. It was business as usual, with all the tradesmen rolling out their tools for the day. The units had been Air Force housing back in the 1960s and 1970s when the local airport was an Air Force Base. But they were now off-base housing for Navy personnel stationed at Point Mugu Naval Air Station, which was about ten miles due south on the Pacific coastline.

As soon as co-workers saw me in my truck, they immediately rushed over—and many offered to hide me since they had all jumped to the conclusion that I was AWOL from the military. I parked my truck and walked over to the main construction office in the job trailer.

As I entered, the project superintendent, who was also a partner in the construction company, looked surprised. Before he had a chance to speak, I handed him my attrition paperwork and began to explain that I had just become the first man ever released from military duty without penalty after being sworn in and that I was not Absent Without Leave from the Navy.

The supervisor said, "How the hell did you do this? Heck, it's probably classified, so you'd better not tell me."

I smiled and said, "You wouldn't believe me if I told you anyway, but you do have the official paperwork in front of you ... so do I still have a job or have you already filled my position?"

"Well, I put an ad in the paper last Monday before you left, but I haven't had any responses yet and we all like you here; so yes, Mr. K, you are lucky enough to be back on the payroll."

"Thank you so much," I said as he turned to the file cabinet to get out my paperwork. "I also like working with the crew and all the subcontractors. You have a great group of people here."

He replied, "You are a part of this group, and we are glad to have you back, but I think you realize this job is winding down in the next few months. I will keep you on until the end, as long as I can, but I have something else to discuss with you. A couple of us, partners of this company, may be splitting off and taking on a huge project in Branson, Missouri. Have you heard of Branson?"

"Yes, sir," I responded. "Branson is supposed to become the new home of the Grand Ole Opry. My father grew up in Mississippi and was childhood friends with a very famous female country singer, so although no one would probably ever suspect, I have country roots in the south and even a little bit of Rebel spirit."

We both laughed and he replied, "I already have contracts in the works for several years of work, and I would like you to move out there and be on my crew. We'll have to see, but there is the possibility that a project manager position will be open."

"Well, sir, as I told the Navy, my priority right now is my son. I am extremely appreciative of the offer, but I would need to think about this for awhile because relocating before obtaining custody would be a bad choice at this point in time."

He replied, "Take your time, and think about it. Things won't get rolling there until about six months after we complete this project. Now, I know you just drove to Oakland and back this weekend in addition to whatever else you had to go through, so do you want a couple of days to regroup before starting back?"

"I am actually anxious to get back to work. I could drive back up the hill and load my tools in my truck and begin today after lunch if you'd like."

To this he said, "Take the rest of the day for yourself; you can roll out tomorrow morning. Oh, and if you want to walk the job right now and say hello to everyone on the site, that's fine. Pretty much all the workers and subs have been asking me how come you left. You have a lot of friends who care about you here. Don't take them away from their work for too long though; most of them are not as productive as you are." He smiled and laughed as he extended his hand to shake mine and said, "Welcome back; see you in the morning."

"Thanks, Al," I told him as I headed out of the job trailer and towards the apartment units currently being remodeled. I made the rounds, popping into each of the units to say, "I'm back, folks." Almost everyone was surprised to see me and wanted to know how I got out of the Navy without being listed as AWOL. I tried to be brief and told them all that I would be starting back tomorrow morning, business as usual.

As I walked back to my truck, I was filled with relief. I had my prevailing wage job back. Al, the project supervisor, had given me a final check that I had not picked up the Friday before. I had to wait three weeks for my next paycheck, so this money would be helpful. I felt things were going so much better than I could have ever expected.

As I started my truck and shifted into reverse to back out of the parking space, the reverse gear made a loud metal-to-metal grinding sound as I released the clutch, which told me my reverse gear was completely gone. In fact, I had to get two guys to help push me back out of the dirt parking spot so I could be on my way. It was almost lunchtime, so I decided to go downtown for a sandwich and beer at a popular local spot. After all, I did have the afternoon off and tomorrow things would be back to the daily routine. I found a parking space along the street where I would not need to use reverse to leave and entered the restaurant.

An hour before noon, the place had just opened and the waitresses were still prepping their stations. I ordered a roast beef and cheddar sandwich on sourdough bread and a Pacifico beer. While I waited for my order, my thoughts were occupied with how I was going to approach my ex-wife about re-establishing shared custody of our son. I was also trying to decide what to do about my truck's transmission. Since the synchro had been out for several months, I already knew it was going to cost more than $3,000 to fix it.

After finishing my sandwich, I ordered a second beer. The restaurant wasn't busy with the lunch crowd yet, so the waitress and I chatted for bit. I told her about my truck problem and asked for her advice, just to keep our conversation going.

She said, "Well, if it were me, and my choices were to spend the money and fix the transmission or buy a new truck, I would buy a new truck if I could afford it."

Just to be flirtatious, I asked her if she wanted to accompany me to the Dodge dealership after work. We both laughed, then I paid the check and left a generous tip.

As I walked across the parking lot to my truck, I realized what a beautiful day it was. It would be nice to take a walk on the beach and just do some thinking. I had given away my surfboards and wetsuit before moving to Ukiah, so paddling out on the ocean wasn't an option, but I thought about driving back up to the house and getting my dog, Pepper. She had been my loyal surf dog since she was six weeks old, and she was almost ten now—but I hadn't taken her to the beach in several weeks now.

I headed for the beach on Highway 101 North—I would be on Old Highway 1 between Ventura and Rincon in fifteen to twenty minutes. As I crossed the bridge over the Santa Clara River between Oxnard and Ventura, I saw the frontage road off-ramp that led to all the car dealerships. Immediately, my left hand lifted the turn signal lever and I exited the freeway with a destination change in mind. Under the bridge, down the frontage road, and into the lot of the Chrysler/Dodge dealership I drove. I turned down the row where the red and white Dakota had been parked about two weeks ago—it was still there, so I parked right in front of it. As I walked up to the driver's door of the new truck, I noticed how small my '87 regular cab looked in comparison to it.

In the distance behind me, I heard a loud voice call out, "How are you today, sir? I'll be right with you."

I turned, saying, "No hurry here, take your time." I recognized the same salesman who had taken me for the test drive almost two weeks ago. He recognized me as well.

He opened with, "What are you doing here? I thought you were joining the Navy. Are you AWOL?" He reached out and shook my hand as he continued, "Great to see you back!"

I began, "You were a little bit upset with me the last time I was here, weren't you? You invest all that time with a customer, think you have a sale, then he tells you he is going into the military for six years. Well, I don't bullshit. I told you I was going to get out of the Navy and come back to buy this truck. Are you still holding that paperwork with the trade-in value of my '87, dealer incentives, and all the bells and whistles as you promised before?" I laughed because my tone sounded overly serious, and I wanted to let him know that I was happy the same salesman was here for me to deal with.

Off to his office we went. An hour later I was in my brand new V8, 4x4, Extra Cab, Dodge Dakota driving south on Highway 101 towards home. How my life had changed in the last few days. All the stress, indecision, drama, trauma, and negativity was absent from my mind. I was free. I had a brand new Dodge truck. I had a really good prevailing wage job. I had dozens of good friends and my family. I felt empowered and almost invincible. I was moving forward with a mindset that I had believed I could never attain again. The only thing I lacked was custody of my son—but that would come about within the next year, another book-long story in itself.

THE SIMPLE MESSAGE
THAT MOST FAIL TO SEE

Mathematics is widely accepted as one of the few true constants in the known universe.

Geometry is mathematics put in physical form for concept and application.

One point stands alone.

Two points establish a line—A to B, a path, distance, destination.

Three points establish a plane—a flat surface, area, common ground.

Four points establish a solid—a physical object, volume. Planes of common ground sharing edges with other planes: interaction & combination forming a solid unit.

Consider the simplest equal-sided solid, a tetrahedron, four isosceles or equilateral triangles forming a triangular pyramid.

A strong structure for its simplicity, it is the building block of higher or more complex polyhedrons.

As the number of symmetrical flat sides increases, so does the strength of the structure to equalized force, however unbalanced or uneven force will weaken the structure.

The symmetrical flat sides become single points as their number approaches infinity, the symmetrical polyhedron object becomes a sphere. Ultimate symmetry. A set of all points equal distance from one center point, able to withstand unbalanced forces with resilient characteristics. Maximized volume, minimized surface area.

From numbers to shapes to words, before time the message has been here right in front of us.

If life exists beyond our short reach in this universe, the message would be the same. Undeniably.

Up or download this to the cranium's conscience and take it out for a couple laps before the race is over.

There is no message in the bottle, blowing smoke is just that, chemical additives decrease performance and longevity only. There is no miracle drug.

The magic, the miracle, the force, the power, the energy is in each and everyone of us—brought to epiphany by experiences. One at a time.

Entropy is a fact, so take charge of your direction because it is not yet possible to change that of time ... Think about it.

Shark2th 09/28/11

About The Author

Shark2th dropped out of college in the early 1980s and started a surfboard factory. He was a computer science major with backgrounds in marine biology, mathematics, physics, chemistry, and more.

A few years later, he returned to working in construction and became a project manager for a company that catered to movie stars and celebrities.

In 1990, he joined the Navy and became the only man in United States history that a President has made an unscheduled flight to meet in the middle of the night during a war. Five months later, he became the first man to ever successfully argue a case to be released from military duty, in order to facilitate becoming one of the first fathers in California to be awarded sole legal and physical custody of a child.